# Contents

# ACKNOWLEDGEMENTS

I would like to thank Sister Andréa of the Missionaries of Charity, Eileen Egan of Catholic Relief Services, Jack Franchetti, Radio and TV Consultant for U.S. Catholic Conference, and Bill Wilson of the Christophers for their help in providing background material for this book. I have also drawn on the following books for some of Mother Teresa's words: Desmond Doig, *Mother Teresa: Her People and Her Work* (New York, 1976); Eileen Egan, *The Works of Peace* (New York, 1965); Georges Gorrée and Jean Barbier, *Love Without Boundaries: Mother Teresa of Calcutta* (Huntington, Indiana, 1976); Ved Mehta, *Portrait of India* (New York, 1970); Malcolm Muggeridge, *Something Beautiful for God* (New York, 1971).

*For My Mother*

# 1
# City of Dreadful Night

Each dawn brings another long day of misery and death to Calcutta. But there is also hope amid the despair, light in the darkness. For when she is in Calcutta, a tiny, slim, slightly-bent woman in her sixties rises at 4:30 A.M. Her lips are thin, her hands are gnarled, her wrinkled skin is the color of ivory, but her small gray-brown eyes have an alert, purposeful look.

She is known as Mother Teresa of Calcutta and, although she is not Indian, after rising she puts on the traditional Indian dress—a white, blue-edged sari of coarse cotton that costs about a dollar. From her left shoulder, fastened by a large safety pin, hangs a crucifix.

After dressing, Mother Teresa will pray and meditate, join in singing the Mass at the motherhouse of the Missionaries of Charity, and then go out into a city that has been called "the slum of the world" to minister to dying beggars, lepers, abandoned children—all of those human beings who are rejected even by the rejected, despised by the despised.

In doing this work from which the most hardened social workers shrink, the tiny woman is putting into practice the call of the prayer of St. Francis of Assisi, "Let me sow love. . . .":

Where there is doubt, faith;
Where there is despair, hope;
Where there is darkness, light;
And where there is sadness, joy.


Mother Teresa herself sees her mission as giving God to the poor in the slums. "Not a dead God," she has said, "but a living, loving God."

The task confronting her is a formidable one which some critics have compared to catching a falling star. Not that all of Calcutta is a ghetto of the poor and unwanted, swollen by millions of refugees from other parts of India. It has always been a city of stark contrasts.

Although Jawaharlal Nehru called Calcutta a "nightmare city," the visitor can see rows of mansions of affluent merchants and grand government buildings lining fashionable Chowringhi Road. Alongside Chowringhi there is an expanse of greenery a mile wide and two miles long. This is the splendid Maidan—the Hyde Park of India—through which horses stabled at the Jodhpur Club canter in the morning.

The Maidan's white marble Victoria Memorial, lakes and well-tended gardens, and monuments to viceroys and soldiers are reminders that from 1774 to 1911 Calcutta was the capital of British India, the second city of the Empire after London, and the first port of Asia.

British Calcutta was known as a "village of palaces," a pleasant home for both sahib and those native Indians who made fortunes from the jute and rice that grow so plentifully in the humid climate. But life in the native *bustis* (slums) where Mother Teresa found her mission always was and still is a symbol for all that seems permanently hopeless in the human condition. Back in 1782, William MacIntosh wrote in his *Travels in Europe, Asia, and Africa*:

> It is a truth that, from the western extremity of California to the eastern coast of Japan, there is not a spot where judgment, taste, decency, and convenience are so grossly insulted as in that scattered and confused chaos of houses, huts, sheds, streets, lanes, alleys, windings, gullies, sinks and tanks, which, jumbled into an undistinguished mass of filth and corruption, equally offensive to human sense and health, compose the capital of the English Company's Government in India. The very small portion of cleanliness which it enjoys is owing to the familiar intercourse of hungry jackals by night, and ravenous vultures, kites, and crows by day.

More than two centuries after MacIntosh's observations, another British writer, the young Rudyard Kipling, found that life in Calcutta had, if anything, gotten worse. Kipling titled his series of articles on Calcutta "The City of Dreadful Night." He was repelled by the all-pervasive stench hanging over the city, which he referred to with the abbreviation B.C.S. (Big Calcutta Stink).

"Stop to consider for a moment," Kipling wrote, "what the cramped compounds, the black soaked soil, the netted intricacies of the service-staircases, and packed stables, the seethment of human life . . . and the curious arrangement of little open drains mean, and you will call it a whited sepulchre."

In his exploration of the city, Kipling encountered

horrors that he felt "cannot be written or hinted at." Yet he found that these horrors were fatalistically accepted as the natural order of things about which nothing could really be done. Today, the horrors have grown steadily worse, although not everyone in Calcutta accepts them with fatalistic resignation. Certainly Mother Teresa does not.

The capital of India was moved to New Delhi in 1911. Since India gained independence in 1947, Calcutta has been only the capital of West Bengal. This is an immense land resembling a steaming swamp, alternately flooded by typhoons or plagued by searing droughts. Its population of about forty-five million is predominantly Hindu in religion. There are about twenty-eight million Hindus, seven million Moslems, two hundred thousand Christians, and a scattering of Buddhists, Sikhs, and Jains.

But the principal problem of West Bengal, and especially of Calcutta, is not the tormenting weather or ancient religious antagonisms, but people. There are, quite simply, too many of them. Calcutta is a living illustration of the so-called "Malthusian nightmare." Malthus, the British economist who wrote more than a century ago, foresaw a world in which man might be doomed to a subsistence existence as the population grew faster than the amount of food that could be grown.

The Calcutta Metropolitan District is an area of 490 square miles in which 8.2 million people try to exist. More than half of them live in Calcutta proper. There are pockets of affluence, with golf courses, race courses, nurses pushing prams in the Maidan, and fashionable clubs like the Turf Club and Swimming Club. There are even scores of literary magazines, for Calcut-

4

ta is the cultural capital of India. Most of the literary magazines are published in Bengali, the language of a people most other Indians consider to be unusually literary and artistic. Calcutta also boasts an active and vibrant theatrical life, with as many as fifteen original plays being performed in Bengali every month.

But the overwhelming majority of Calcutta's residents do not attend the plays or read the literary journals. They are illitcrate and simply try to survive in the *bustis* where two things are ever-present: a smell combined of human sweat, excrement, urine, cow dung, incense, and jasmine, and beggars' cries of *"Baksheesh! Baksheesh!"* ("Alms!")

In the *bustis*, few buildings are more than three stories high. Most are one or two story structures made of unbaked bricks, bamboo, or mud with no inside plumbing. They are under permanent siege from mosquitoes, flies, and vermin that breed, carry, and spread disease.

The worst time is the monsoon season from mid-June to September. Warm rains break every dawn and blow off the Bay of Bengal, flooding sewers and latrines, swamping mud hovels, turning the muddy streets into streams carrying garbage and excrement. Tuberculosis, smallpox, malaria, cholera, typhus, and dysentery are rampant. The always thin line between life and death begins to break down. The monsoon season becomes the season of death in the *bustis* of Calcutta.

At least a million people sleep on the sidewalks at night. Thousands of the skin-and-bones starving, so far gone that they are refused admission to the crowded hospitals, die on the sidewalks. Newborn babies are found on garbage heaps. Leprous beggars without hands or feet or noses whimper for *baksheesh*. Wet, coughing children beg with tin cups.

Both foreigner and native become inured to this unchanging scene of incoherent despair, of unremitting human desolation, and turn away from these "poorest of the poor." It is not true, however, that nobody cares. The Ford Foundation studies ways to relieve the grinding poverty. The Calcutta Metropolitan Development Authority plans numerous transit, sewerage, and slum clearance projects. The World Bank advances millions of dollars for water purification, sanitation, and drainage. India harvested about one hundred and twenty million tons of grain in 1976, but also received six hundred thousand tons in aid from the United States. In New Delhi, the Indian Government's Ministry for Health and Family Planning announces a new program to slow the explosive population growth by raising the minimum marriage age and paying more money to people who voluntarily have themselves sterilized.

But none of these well-meant plans or projects seem to relieve the misery; their pace only equals the pace of deterioration. While Indians in Calcutta rarely exhibit conscious and deliberate cruelty, they do exhibit an indifference toward their fellow man, an absence of any social sense that extends beyond their own religious, ethnic, family, or caste group. So as charts are drawn and statistics are compiled, individual human beings continue to die in the streets of Calcutta, unmourned, unwanted, forgotten by Indians of any means at all in a city that seems beyond redemption or hope. One remembers Lenin's dictum: "The road to world revolution leads through Peking, Shanghai, and Calcutta."

The dying are not forgotten, however, by Mother

Teresa. "We want them to know that there are people who really love them, who really want them, at least for the few hours that they have to live, to know human and divine love," she has said. The work of this small woman and the Sisters of the Missionaries of Charity, the order she founded in 1950, embodies the concept of Christian love in action. But it is work which, for understandable reasons, few would choose.

On a typical morning, Mother Teresa, after Mass at the motherhouse of the Missionaries of Charity at 54A Lower Circular Road, gets into an ambulance with ten of her nuns—some of them high-caste Indian ladies who have chosen to join the order.

The ambulance drives to one of the *bustis*. Emaciated figures in rags can be seen raking over piles of garbage in search of something to eat. One man can be seen dragging himself along a steaming sidewalk. His vocal cords are so damaged that his plea for alms resembles an unintelligible sob. His face is ulcerated. His left hand looks like a claw; his right hand is a stump.

Mother Teresa sees the other ragged, stick-like figures shrink back to make way for him and realizes that he is a leper, one of perhaps 300,000 in the Calcutta area. No one will employ these lepers; no one will come near them or help them. They inspire revulsion and fear of contagion.

Mother Teresa has the ambulance stop next to the man, who has stopped crawling. She and four other nuns get out of the ambulance, surround the leper, pick him up, and carry him into the ambulance. There they sponge the maggot-bloated lesions covering his body.

The ambulance drives to Dhapa at the southeast limits of Calcutta. Dhapa is the site of the city's huge

7

refuse dump. There is also a slaughterhouse there, desolate encampments of the poor, and women scavenging in the rubbish heaps.

One of the many leper camps operated by the Missionaries of Charity in India is located in this bleak landscape. The camp consists of rows of clay or stone huts and a modern clinic. Vultures circle overhead. Wild dogs roam everywhere.

Mother Teresa deposits the man at the clinic, where he can be given food and medical attention. Then she walks through the muddy main street of the camp. Lepers crowd around her, crying *"Mataji, Mataji"* (Mother) and *"Jesu pranam"* (Praise be to Jesus). She touches some of them reassuringly, offers an encouraging word in Bengali to others. But she knows that many of them will not survive the hideous disease that afflicts them and that many others, because they lack education, will leave the camp before the leprosy can be arrested      .

However, she also knows that those who do die while in the care of the Missionaries of Charity will be given a decent death and the only measure of love they have ever known. Mother Teresa believes, with Saint Francis, that "it is in giving that we receive" and that "it is in dying that we are born to eternal life."

Mother Teresa and the Missionaries of Charity translate these beliefs into action every day after Mass. In doing so, they serve as the instruments of charity of Catholics and non-Catholics all over the world, although the task facing all missionaries in India is staggering. After China, India is the world's most populous country with about 653 million inhabitants. Each dawn, as the hot Indian sun begins to rise over this vast land, there are about 35,000 more people living there than there were the previous day—a population growth that often breeds despair and suffering. But each morning about a thousand Missionaries of Charity go out to give the love of Christ by trying to relieve despair and suffering. Given the gap between their numbers and those of the poor, it might seem improbable that their efforts could have any real impact or meaning. But then it might also seem improbable for Mother Teresa to be working in India at all. Her spiritual journey to Calcutta began more than six decades ago and thousands of miles away in a tiny land where the practice of Christianity is now forbidden by the state.

# 2
# Letters from a Jesuit

"God moves in a mysterious way His wonders to perform." So wrote the poet William Cowper. Indeed, there is a certain mystery, until one understands the connecting links, in how a peasant girl from an obscure, non-Catholic Balkan country could cross thousands of miles to the vast subcontinent of India and become Mother Teresa of Calcutta.

Mother Teresa was born Agnes Gonxha Bejaxhiu on August 27, 1910 in Skopje. This ancient city was then part of Albania, one of the small and backward countries of the Balkan peninsula in southeastern Europe across the Adriatic Sea from Italy.

Skopje and its surrounding province of Macedonia is a hard but ruggedly beautiful land that has been fought over by Illyrians, Romans, Byzantines, Slavs, and Turks. The Turks overran Skopje in 1392, made it into a commercial center, and called it Uskup or Uskub.

When Agnes was born in 1910 her native city was part of the Turkish Ottoman Empire. It was cold in winter and very hot in summer. Standing on both banks of the Vardar River, Skopje was dominated by an old Turkish fortress on a hill and the huge and graceful mosque of Mustapha Pasha, built in 1492.

The mosque had intricate geometric patterns on its

walls, precious carpets on its floors, and a clock which kept Mecca time. Nearby was the Orthodox Church of Sveti Spas (Saint Savior). It was much smaller than the mosque, for the Turks did not want it to detract from the mosque's glory. But Saint Savior did contain an artistic treasure in its iconostasis—the partition which divides the church from the altar—of carved walnut depicting scenes from biblical history.

A child growing up in the Skopje of the early twentieth century would walk through narrow cobbled streets lined with tiny houses and the shops and stalls of craftsmen. Each street had its own specialty—basketmaking, shoemaking, metal working; there was even a street for lawyers. There were Turkish baths, a gypsy quarter, dozens of mosques, and the Kursumli Han, a massive old Turkish caravanserai with dozens of cubicles for travelers. In the narrow streets businessmen in conventional Western dress could be seen, as well as Albanians in white skull caps, peasants in thick black homespun, gypsy women in baggy pantaloons of vivid design, and Turks wearing the fez.

There were more than a hundred monasteries in the mountains around Skopje, although the Turks had allowed many of them to crumble into ruin during the long centuries of their reign. But while the Turks ruled firmly, they did not forbid the practice of Christianity by their Orthodox and Roman Catholic minorities. However, when Agnes was two years old, in 1912, the first Balkan War broke out in Macedonia and a year later Skopje was liberated from the Turks and incorporated by treaty into Serbia. After further fighting in World War I, it was made part of the new nation of Yugoslavia in 1918.

Today Skopje is the capital of Macedonia, one of

the six federated republics which make up Communist Yugoslavia. There are few Turks left. Both monasteries and mosques are closed, or are open simply as historic sites. Nor is Skopje physically the same city in which Agnes Gonxha Bejaxhiu passed the first eighteen years of her life. Thirty-five years after she had left, this city of 200,000 people was struck, in July 1963, by an earthquake that ruined eighty percent of it.

But Agnes, born of Albanian peasant stock, spent —by her own account—a happy childhood in ancient Skopje in a family of two girls and one boy. Her religious vocation had its origins within her family. "I think it began at home with our people, with my own family," she has said. "I was only a child then, and especially my mother was very devoted to Jesus in the Eucharist. And I remember when I was living home she said, 'Put your hand in His—in His Hand—and walk all the way along with Him.' So she knew what was expected of one who gives her life to Jesus totally."

By the age of twelve, Agnes wanted to be a missionary, "to go out and give the love of Christ." While attending the government school, she joined the Sodality. Yugoslav Jesuits had been sent to work in the Calcutta Archdiocese in 1925. One of these Jesuits sent back letters about the Bengal mission field. Agnes listened to these enthusiastic letters when they were read regularly to the sodality, and they aroused her interest in doing missionary work in India.

In 1925, India seemed to be a firmly fixed part of the British Empire—so much so that most people forgot that the Roman Catholic Church, and the Jesuits in particular, were active in India long before the British took control of the subcontinent.

Greece, Rome, Venice, and Genoa had all come

briefly to India to trade, but Portugal was the first Western country to come and stay on more than an economic basis. Four ships under Vasco da Gama, sent by the King of Portugal, landed near Calicut on May 17, 1498, 114 years before the British East India Company built its first warehouse in Western India.

Da Gama said that he had come to seek "Christians and spices." And indeed he found both, for Christianity was in India, brought from the Middle East, before it was in Rome. Small sects of Christians lived among the Hindus and Moslems. Tradition had it, though historical evidence was lacking, that the first Indian converts were made by the disciple Thomas himself soon after the crucifixion.

Now these Christians were rediscovered by da Gama. Within a year after his arrival, regular trade was established between Portugal and Cochin. A fort housing a Portuguese governor and 1,500 soldiers was built at Cochin in 1503.

But the Portuguese were concerned with more than trade and military conquest. Like the Spaniards of the time in the Americas, Catholicism was part of their cultural being. The Portuguese were both crusaders and traders, and they carried their Catholicism with them wherever they went. European trade with India was held by the papacy to be the province of the Catholic King of Portugal, as were Christian missions and the eternal salvation of Indians.

In May 1542, the Basque Francis Xavier arrived at the port of Goa on the west coast, the capital of Portuguese India, after a 4,000 mile sea voyage from Lisbon. Francis Xavier, as a university student in Paris, had become a close friend of Ignatius Loyola. In 1534, Xavier and five others joined Loyola in taking the vow

13

of perpetual poverty and chastity to form the nucleus of the Society of Jesus to work "for the greater glory of God."

Immediately after arriving in Goa with a brief as papal nuncio, Francis Xavier began to preach with remarkable success. Francis faced formidable obstacles in Hindu Brahminism with its caste system, Islam with its hostility to things Christian, and the rapacity and immorality of many of the Portuguese colonials.

But Francis was not deterred and, in bringing the word of one true God to the pluralistic society of India, he preached to all levels of that society. He added a new dimension to missionary work by going among those who were neglected or despised by both the Portuguese officials and their own native rulers. Francis lived in a public hospital, ministered to the sick and dying, and begged from door to door in Goa for the needs of paupers, prisoners, lepers, and the outcast diseased.

As more Jesuits came to India, Francis assigned them to missions he had started. In the Goa area, headquarters for the Jesuits in India, 12,967 baptisms were recorded in 1560 alone. Saint Francis, who became known as the Apostle to the Indies, traveled many thousands of miles throughout Asia in eleven years. He preached in Japan, died in 1552 while attempting to enter China, and is buried in Goa.

Franciscans, Augustinians, Dominicans, and Carmelites followed the Jesuits, one of whose most intriguing members was the Italian Roberto de Nobili. He arrived in Goa from Portugal in 1605 and went to work in Madurai, in South India.

De Nobili soon conceived the revolutionary idea that to bring Christianity to the Indians it would be necessary to penetrate Indian thought and adapt to Indian customs. The Jesuit discovered that the way of life most resembling that of a priest was practiced by a small group of men known as *sannyāsīs* who were devoted to the contemplation of God and the problems of philosophy. Accordingly, de Nobili took up the garb and the way of life of the *sannyāsīs*.

Instead of coming as a foreigner, the Jesuit wandered through the interior of India living on alms, eating one meal a day of rice and herbs, carrying a bamboo stick and a gourd of water, wearing a thin cloth of red-ochre cotton, and preaching to all castes, including the poorest and most despised. De Nobili mastered Tamil, a native Dravidian language, and was the first European to learn Sanskrit and to study the *Vedas*, the oldest scriptures of Hinduism. He extracted from the *Vedas*, which were some 2,500 years old, a collection of allusions and texts suited to serve as a basis for demonstrating the truth of Christianity.

De Nobili made thousands of converts, not just in the coastal enclaves but in the interior as well, and won the respect of the Indians, who accorded him the title of *guru*—spiritual teacher and master. However, the Jesuit's unorthodox methods aroused the hostility of some of his superiors who felt that his bringing Christianity to the Indians in terms they could understand verged on heresy and schism. A celebrated controversy ensued for thirteen years in ecclesiastical courts until de Nobili's approach was approved by Pope Gregory XV.

But by the time Father de Nobili died in India in 1656, known to Hindus and Christians alike as *o santo Padre*, the era of Portuguese domination, and with it the exclusive character of Catholic missionary activity, was over. Portugal, a kingdom of less than a million people, did not have the resources to maintain vast empires in Asia, Africa, and Latin America.

The Portuguese were replaced in India by the Dutch, who were in turn displaced by the English. But Western missionaries, both Protestant and Catholic, continued to trickle into India. The trickle increased to a flood in the late nineteenth and early twentieth centuries. The missionaries founded churches, schools for the blind, insane asylums, hospitals, homes for lepers, agricultural institutes, schools and colleges. But when Agnes heard the letters written from India by the Yugoslav Jesuit read to her sodality in Skopje, it was apparent that still more work was needed to improve the physical life of the people. And only about two percent of the people of India were Christians.

Agnes decided to volunteer for the Bengal Mission and she was put in touch with some nuns of the Institute of the Blessed Virgin Mary, or Ladies of Loretto. This community of religious women, popularly known by names such as Loretto Nuns, *Englischen Fräulein* and *Dami Inglesi* depending on the countries where they taught, was established in 1609. Mother Mary Ward and seven companions had then founded a boarding school for English Catholic refugees, and a free day school, at Saint Omer, Flanders. The purpose of the order was the instruction of youth. The order adopted the rule of the Jesuits.

The Institute of the Blessed Virgin Mary spread to England, Italy, Austria, Germany, and France and later to Africa, Australia, South America, the United States, and India. There are now houses on every continent. The Institute's educational work, extending from primary school to university, prepares Catholic women to fulfill roles as lay apostles.

In 1821, Mary Ball had founded a house in Dublin. India later became one of the Irish generalate's provinces. Some of the Irish nuns were teaching in the Calcutta Archdiocese when Agnes volunteered for the Bengal mission. To prepare her for this work, she was sent on November 29, 1928 to the Loretto Abbey at Rathfarnham, a suburb southwest of Dublin. Rathfarnham is also the site of the Jesuit House of Studies in what was once an Elizabethan castle and the influential bilingual St. Enda's School. St. Enda's was founded in 1910 as part of the Gaelic movement by Padraic Pearse, who commanded the Irish forces in the 1916 Easter Rebellion and was executed by the British.

This austere Irish setting must have seemed like a great change for Agnes from the backward but colorful life of Skopje. After preparation at the Loretto Abbey, she was sent to India to begin her novitiate. She arrived in Calcutta on January 6, 1929. Agnes Gonxha Bejaxhiu had at last reached that vast, diverse and—to Westerners—often baffling and daunting land in which she had wanted to serve ever since hearing the letters of the Yugoslav Jesuit read to her sodality. She was ready to "to go out and give the love of Christ," although no one could know then what a unique form that giving would eventually take.

But then St. Francis Xavier himself, when he set sail from Lisbon, did not know what awaited him in India.

# 3
# The Call

Although she landed at Calcutta, Agnes had no chance to tour the city. The young novice was sent immediately by train some two hundred miles north to the Loretto Convent at Darjeeling in the Himalayan foothills.

Whatever she expected to find in India, Agnes found in Darjeeling an unlikely setting for missionary work. Under the British Raj, Darjeeling was a cool and pleasant hill station and resort. The Governor of Bengal and his staff went there to escape the searing summer heat of Calcutta. So did some affluent Indian businessmen.

In Darjeeling, Agnes saw towering snow-capped mountains that reminded her of the countryside around Skopje. She could see the ranges of Bhutan and Sikkim and, nearby, the magnificent twin peaks of Mount Kanchenjuga. Mountain climbing could be undertaken with local *sherpas* (guide-porters). Mount Everest, still unconquered in 1929, was 140 miles away.

Darjeeling was built on three levels connected by almost vertical lanes and flights of steps. Nepalese, Bhutias, Lepchas, and Tibetans, all wearing colorful tribal costumes, lived and worked on the two lower levels. The narrow but clean streets were jammed with exotic bazaars and market places and small Indian hotels and restaurants.

The first level was the preserve of the British Raj. Here there were fine hotels, cafes and shops, the blue-domed Government House, and comfortable villas staffed by many Indian servants and equipped with electric fans and refrigerators. There was a mall for promenading and riding, dining and dancing at the Gymkhana, a stoppage of work at tea time, and a small racecourse that was described as the highest in the world.

As in the rest of British India, social relations between officials and soldiers and natives were extremely rare. The civil servant who was interested in Indian culture or religions was even rarer. Despite the efforts of missionaries to convert them to Christianity, the religion of the masses, whether Hindu or Moslem, remained largely untouched.

Some of the British tried to break down the barriers between themselves and the natives, but few met with success. There was some public fraternization, but mainly with those Indians—princely rulers and affluent businessmen—who had little identification with the masses. The British sense of moral superiority to the Indian population—ninety percent of whom could not read or write and whose numbers increased by nearly one hundred million from 1880 to 1930—expressed itself in disdain and sometimes open contempt.

In turn, the widespread economic and social discontent beyond the comfortable confines of Darjeeling crystallized in a nationalist struggle that was gaining considerable force. In December 1929 the Indian National Congress, the principal nationalist movement led by Mahatma Gandhi, declared that its aim was not

19

Dominion status but complete independence. In April 1930 Gandhi inaugurated a civil disobedience campaign to achieve that end.

At the Loretto Convent in Darjeeling, it was possible to be completely unaware of these developments or of the misery of the Indian masses. But then Agnes had not come to India to involve herself in political movements, and she never would. Nor had she come to India to convert Indians, and she would never claim to be a learned theologian. It would, in any case, have taken a European like Roberto de Nobili to master the subtleties and complexities of Hinduism.

Hinduism, in which eighty-five percent of the Indian population believed, was both an ancient civilization and a conglomerate of religions. It had neither a beginning, nor a founder, nor a hierarchy nor central authority. The core of Hinduism did not even depend on the existence of God or on whether there was one God or many gods.

One of the characteristics of Hinduism which a Western newcomer like Agnes could not escape noticing, however, was the caste system. Hindu society was a complex division of nearly 3,000 castes and subcastes, but there were four principal social classes.

The *Brāhmana* (Brahmins) were regarded as the highest of all human beings. They were teachers and the guardians and dispensers of divine power. The *Ksatriya* (nobles) were warriors whose main duties were to protect the people and to provide gifts and food for the Brahmins. The third caste, the *Vaiśyas*, were destined to tend cattle, to trade, and to cultivate land. The fourth caste, the *Sūdras*, had the sole duty of "serving meekly" the three upper castes with offerings of labor.

The untouchables lived outside the caste system. Those in the castes considered them to be unclean.

Merely to touch them was seen as defiling.

The thoroughgoing inequality and exclusiveness of the castes shocked Western missionaries. Gandhi was doing what he could to end discrimination against the untouchables, whom he called the "Children of God." The British, however much they might be accused of exploiting a colony for economic gain by Indian nationalists, had managed to put an end to some unpleasant practices they found on the subcontinent. These included slavery, female infanticide, child marriage, the burning of widows, and the depredations of the Thug gangs who murdered and robbed in the name of the goddess Kali. But the British had a general policy of non-intervention in religious and social matters. The Raj declined to play either the Hindu ruler's role of enforcing caste distinctions or the reformer's role of abolishing them.

As a result, no one was really trying to ease the plight of the poorest of the poor when Agnes arrived in India. But then she had not been sent to India as a social worker by her order. She fully accepted her role as a Roman Catholic teaching nun who hoped only in some yet undefined way to "give the love of Christ." So she gladly took up the teaching of well-to-do European children and some Indians at the Loretto Convent in Darjeeling, far removed from the harsh realities of Calcutta.

Agnes never had any doubts that she had done the right thing in becoming a nun. "It was the will of God," she has said. "It was His choice." She loved teaching above everything else. There was no reason to suspect that she would not continue indefinitely in that valuable vocation, as thousands of Loretto nuns had done before her.

The young novice took her first vows at Darjeeling

on May 24, 1931 and the name Teresa. The choice was inspired by the example of St. Thérèse of Lisieux (1873-97), the French Carmelite nun who is the patroness of aviators and missionaries and who is known as the "Little Flower of Jesus." Thérèse was a simple nun in an obscure convent who exemplified the "little way"—achieving goodness by performing the humblest tasks and carrying out the most trivial action. She was proclaimed "the greatest saint of modern times" by Pope Pius XI.

After taking her first vows, Sister Teresa was sent to teach at the Loretto Convent in the Entally district of Calcutta. Inside the convent wall were well-kept school buildings surrounded by green lawns. One of the buildings housed Saint Mary's, in whose yellow-washed rooms cloistered nuns in white habits taught Bengali girls in their own language. Most of them came from affluent Calcutta homes. The vast majority of Indian girls did not go to school after the age of nine, if at all.

Sister Teresa taught geography at Saint Mary's and later became its principal. She was also in charge of the Daughters of Saint Anne, the Indian religious order attached to the Loretto sisters. In 1937, she took her final vows as a Loretto nun.

Life inside the convent wall was pleasant, protected, and rewarding. But just outside the convent wall Sister Teresa could not help but notice the *Moti Jheel*. For one thing, there was the stench from nearby tanneries. There were also man-made mountains of reeking refuse dumps. The *Moti Jheel* was one of the most congested and miserable slums in Calcutta and Sister Teresa could see it from the terrace of Saint Mary's. One day she went outside the convent wall and walked through the narrow, filthy lanes of the *Moti Jheel* (Pearl Lake).

Here was a world quite different from Skopje, the quiet of the Loretto Abbey in the green hills south of Dublin, and the peace of the Loretto Convent in the cool, clean surroundings of the Himalayan foothills. In the *Moti Jheel*, human beings lived in bamboo and earth-plastered shacks with sagging tin roofs and no sanitation. Many thousands of others slept in railway stations or under mud walls or out in the open on mats of banana leaves. Those fortunate enough to have a small diet of rice did their cooking on stoves fueled by molded cakes of cow dung. But there were many who had nothing to eat at all and they simply died of starvation in the stinking lanes. There were other sights . . . vultures waiting to descend upon emaciated but still breathing bodies, living fetuses thrown to dogs to eat, infants nursing at their mothers' shriveled breasts.

Sister Teresa came back inside the convent wall but she could not forget what she had seen. She returned to the *Moti Jheel* and then visited the other slums of Calcutta. The slums were not isolated in any one quarter, but were interspersed with the solid and often vibrant business and residential sections of Calcutta. The slums could not be overlooked. Nevertheless, the more fortunate Indians and the British Raj seemed to accept them with resignation. But something had to be done for these people, Sister Teresa thought.

She asked permission of her superiors to go out into the slums and it was granted. Accompanied by girls from the Sodality of Our Lady, students at the convent school ranging in age from twelve to twenty, she went to hospitals to comfort the sick and into the narrow lanes of the slums with the few bandages, aspirins, and bottles of iodine she could obtain. Prayer without action is no prayer at all, Sister Teresa believed, and she has said: "Faith in action is love and love in action is service."

But as the years went by and World War II ended and the nationalists demand for the independence of India grew more impatient and violent, conditions in the slums did not change. Sister Teresa, maintaining a full teaching schedule in the convent school, did what she could when she could to relieve the suffering during her visits outside. But it did not seem to be enough. She was happy teaching, although she began to see life in the convent, even with its vows of poverty, obedience, and chastity, as unduly easeful compared to life in the slums. The appalling conditions there were beginning to disturb her increasingly.

But what could one person do, especially a cloistered nun in a convent with no resources?

On September 10, 1946, Sister Teresa traveled by train to make her annual retreat at the Loretto Convent in Darjeeling. She did not sleep much during the overnight journey. As the wheels of the train hammered rhythmically, she could not keep visions of what she had seen in the slums from her mind. It was on that train ride to Darjeeling that she heard an inner voice and made a decision.

"I heard the call to give up all and follow Him into the slums," she remembers, "to serve Him among the poorest of the poor. I knew that it was His will, and that I had to follow Him. There was no doubt that it was going to be His work."

Sister Teresa decided to go out into the streets to serve the poorest of the poor on a full-time basis. "It was a call within my vocation," she has said. "It was a second calling."

In later years, Sister Teresa would describe her purpose in these terms: "We are missionaries to bring God's love and compassion into the world of today. That very fact, that we bring the hungry and the naked and the homeless and the dying, that we take care of them, is because Jesus has said so. And He cannot deceive us and He said very clearly: 'You did it to Me and I was hungry and you fed Me.' And to make sure that we understand what He meant, He took that as a point on which we are going to be judged at the end of our life. That I was hungry and you fed me or I was hungry and you didn't feed me. And it's something very beautiful that Christ didn't mean only the hunger for bread but He meant that hunger for love, for human dignity, for understanding love, for compassion."

But before she could transform such thoughts into action, Sister Teresa first had to ask permission of the Archbishop of Calcutta, Ferdinand Périer, to leave the Loretto convent and work exclusively among the poor. Upon her return to Calcutta from the retreat at Darjeeling, Sister Teresa did make that request. For the time, it was highly unusual. In 1946, nuns who had taken final vows were not permitted to leave a convent. It was also one thing to serve the poor from a convent, and another actually to merge with the poor.

Archbishop Périer refused Sister Teresa's request. Since she would never have questioned ecclesiastical authority, her unusual mission might never have begun. But because of the determination and patience of this frail, thirty-six-year-old nun who had heard an inner voice, it did begin.

# 4
# An Answer from Rome

In 1947, British India at last became independent but only after being partitioned into India and Pakistan, a separate Moslem state. The flight of those Moslem and Hindu groups which suddenly found themselves in hostile territory was accompanied by savage riots in which at least 200,000 people were killed. From seven to eight million people fled from Pakistan to India. Bengal, because it had both Hindu and Moslem populations, was split into West and East Bengal. The former became a state of the Republic of India and the latter made up the eastern wing of Pakistan. Millions of Hindus left East Bengal and poured into the already overcrowded new capital of West Bengal, Calcutta. Most of the newcomers were homeless, penniless, jobless, and hungry. Kipling's "City of Dreadful Night" became a nightmare city.

Sister Teresa continued teaching at the Loretto convent, but she also continued her work outside in the teeming slums. It had now become more urgently needed than ever, and so she repeated her request to Archbishop Périer.

The Archbishop, who was in his eighties, reconsidered the unusual request. He was still dubious, but realized that the work that Sister Teresa wanted to do was needed. "If it is needed, then God will bless it," he told another priest. The Archbishop suggested that Sister Teresa ask permission of the Mother General of the Loretto nuns to leave the convent and then, if it was granted, to write to the Pope for permission.

The Mother General responded to the request with the observation: "If God is calling you, I give you permission with all my heart. I want you to know that we love you, and if you ever want to come back to us, there will always be a place for you."

Sister Teresa then wrote to Pope Pius XII in the spring of 1948. In her letter, she said that she had a vocation and that God was calling her to give up all and to surrender herself to Him in the service of the poorest of the poor in the slums.

She received an answer from Rome by return post on April 12, 1948. The Pope granted her request "to live alone outside the cloister among the poor of Calcutta, with God alone as protector and guide." She could do her work as an unenclosed nun under obedience to the Archbishop of Calcutta.

But even though she had now received permission, Sister Teresa faced overwhelming obstacles to carrying out her vocation. She had no money, no helpers, no medical training, and no place to work and live. She was literally alone, except for one thing: faith in the love of Jesus and a powerful determination to translate His love into action.

The French historian and statesman, Alexis de Tocqueville, writing in his *Democracy in America* in 1835, expressed the concept of modern man lost "in the solitude of his own heart." The concept grew, and in our own times is expressed in such terms as "alienation," "the mass man," and "the lonely crowd." Modern man and woman are seen as creatures uprooted by industrialism, jammed into cities with people they don't know, adrift on a sea of lost spiritual values, alone and helpless against huge bureaucracies, bewildering and massive economic and political changes, unable to do anything about such seemingly insoluble problems as hunger, sickness, despair, and loneliness of the spirit. But Sister Teresa, who did not feel alone, acted as though she did not accept or was not even aware of these concepts.

In August 1948, after exchanging the Loretto habit in which she had worked so happily for a white cotton sari with a blue border and a crucifix pinned on the left shoulder, Sister Teresa traveled some 240 miles northwest to Patna. This city of 500,000 people, most of whom were Moslems, was once the capital of an empire that had lasted from 500 B.C. to 500 A.D. and was one of the envies of the ancient world.

In Patna, Sister Teresa undertook intensive nursing training with the American Medical Missionary Sisters. In December she returned to Calcutta and went to live in one small room provided by the Little Sisters of the Poor. Four days before Christmas, 1948, she opened her first school in the *Moti Jheel*.

The school was an open space among huts without benches, chairs, or blackboards. The students were from the streets, and although they were big children, they had never been to school. Sister Teresa taught them the Bengali alphabet by writing it in the mud with a stick and also gave much-needed lessons in hygiene. There were five students on the first day.

But with faith, came help.

"The next day two or three girls came from the school where I taught to help," Sister Teresa has said. "Gradually the work started to grow and some ladies from Calcutta who had been teachers in the school where I had been teaching also came. At first, I had only five rupees, but gradually, as people came to know what I was doing, they brought things and money."

In February 1949, a Catholic priest went to the house of Michael Gomes, an Indian civil servant in the teaching profession and a Catholic, to give the Last Sacraments to his seriously ill mother. The Gomes family lived in a large ancestral house, slightly run-down, on Creek Lane near the *Moti Jheel*. Two of the four Gomes brothers had left the house and the entire upper floor was empty.

The visiting priest mentioned Sister Teresa and her work to Michael Gomes, a slim, shy man who wears eyeglasses, and wondered if he knew of a place where she might find living quarters. Michael Gomes offered the use of the upper floor. But it was too big and Sister Teresa eventually moved into one room, bringing with her all she had—a chair, a packing-case which served as a desk, and a suitcase.

Michael Gomes, considered to be a very holy man by Sister Teresa, would never accept any money from her for rent or food.

Sister Teresa's first postulant came next, on March 19, 1949. She was Subhasini Das, a small, quiet Bengali girl who had been one of Sister Teresa's students at the Loretto convent. Subhasini Das assumed the Christian name Agnes when she took her vows. Others followed Sister Agnes.

"The first ten girls who came in were all students that I had taught in the school," Sister Teresa remembers. "One by one they surrendered themselves to God to serve the poorest of the poor. They wanted to give their all to God. Then other helpers came: doctors and nurses came on a voluntary basis to help us."

Those were hard days for Sister Teresa and the first eleven girls who joined her, Manuel Gomes recalls. They rose at 5:30 A.M., prayed and attended Mass, and by 7:30 A.M. were out in the streets, bringing what food they could to the poor, comforting the sick in hospitals, teaching. "They used to go begging from door to door," says Mr. Gomes, "and there were people who just turned their backs. But God helped them. It came. It came. Something always turns up."

On October 7, 1950 the new diocesan congregation of the Missionaries of Charity, approved by the Pope, was instituted in Calcutta. There were still only twelve members, and the foundress was now known as Mother Teresa. Her concept of the structure of the new congregation was simple: "To quench the thirst of Jesus Christ on the Cross for love of souls by the Sisters' observance of the four vows of poverty, chastity, obedience, and charity."

The sisters had their heads shaved, they all wore the white cotton sari with a blue border, and they never went out into the slums alone but in pairs. Mother Teresa has always firmly insisted: "We are not social workers, though we do social work." Sister Agnes, who became her assistant, has said: "Every day we have Mass, half an hour of meditation, morning prayer, afternoon prayer, and in the evening we have a full hour of Adoration. It would not be possible to work otherwise. There must be a spiritual motive. You can work only for God. You can never work for any man."

The little community continued to grow. Most of its novices were middle-class Indian girls, but some came from the richer and higher class and there were also many Anglo-Indian girls.

"From the day they join the community," Mother Teresa has explained, "we spend a very good deal of time in training the Sisters, especially in the spirit and life of the society which is beautifully defined in the constitution. This is the written will of God for us. Also, side by side with the spiritual training, they have to go to the slums. Slum work and this meeting with the people are a part of the novitiate training. This is something special to us as a congregation because as a rule novices do not go out, but to be able to understand the meaning of our fourth vow, which promises that we give our wholehearted free service to the poorest of the poor—to Christ in his distressing disguise—because of this it is necessary that they come face to face with the reality, so as to be able to understand what their life is going to be, when they will have taken their vows and when they will have to meet Christ twenty-four hours a day in the poorest of the poor in the slums."

Girls volunteered for the Missionaries of Charity as aspirants and spent about six months observing their work. "They have to see if this is what God wants for them," Mother Teresa has said. "And we have to see if they really have a vocation for this kind of life and work. At the same time they have to learn English because that is the language of our community, and as we do not have enough spiritual books in Indian languages we have to use English books. Also, in India we have so many languages, and the Sisters come from all over India, so it would be very difficult to train them in spiritual life if there are so many languages being used in one community; so because of all this we have decided to use English. After that they have to spend six months in postulancy where they begin to learn the rudiments of spiritual life. After these six months they join the novitiate for two years. During that time they have an intensive spiritual training in theology, Church history and the Scriptures, and especially in the rules and the constitution of our community. Because the Sisters are going to bind themselves by vows, they must know exactly what these vows are going to mean to them. The vow of poverty is very, very strict in our congregation because to be able to love the poor and to know the poor we must be poor ourselves."

The strictness of these rules seemed to encourage rather than discourage aspirants. When the Missionaries of Charity was made a diocesan congregation in October 1950 it became obvious that they would need larger living quarters. They now occupied the entire upper floor of the Gomes house in Creek Lane and, in the memory of a local priest, "were sleeping side by side like sardines and praying to get a permanent house."

Mother Teresa made a novena to Saint Cecilia. At about this time a wealthy Moslem decided to move to Pakistan, and he put his house up for sale. It was on the same street as the Church of Saint Teresa, whose pastor, Father Henry, had ministered to the Bengali community since coming to India from Belgium in 1938. Father Henry knew Sister Teresa well and was one of her most fervent champions. He went to see the Moslem gentleman and found that he had been educated by Jesuits. The Moslem offered to sell his house for less than the price of the land.

The Archbishop of Calcutta approved the purchase. The Missionaries of Charity now had a mother-house. It was really three houses with a courtyard at 54A Lower Circular Road in the center of Calcutta. The street is noisy and crowded with pedestrians. The rattling of streetcars mingles with the prayers being said at 54A Lower Circular Road which—though a chapel has been added and other enlargements have been made since 1950—remains the motherhouse of the Missionaries of Charity.

From the new motherhouse, Mother Teresa went out into the streets and encountered a sight which both shocked and inspired her with compassion. People—sick, starving, penniless—were dying in the streets and simply being left there to die, alone. The bustling life of Calcutta went on around them, and nobody seemed to care.

But what could one individual do to stem this flood of misery? What, for that matter could the Republic of India or the Calcutta Corporation, the governing body of the city, do? The destitute who slept on benches, in parks, on sidewalks, and on the platforms of railroad stations couldn't all be arrested for loitering or vagrancy. The jails and hospitals were already jammed. And as dispensaries and soup kitchens were set up, and some medicine and clothing were sent into the slums by international relief organizations and the Indian government, the homeless, jobless, penniless, starving refugees kept flooding in from East Pakistan, forming an ocean that inundated the relief efforts.

One day in 1954 Mother Teresa found a woman lying on the pavement in front of a Calcutta hospital. The woman was dying, but she was so far gone that she seemed oblivious to the rats and ants gnawing at her wizened feet. Mother Teresa picked up the emaciated woman and carried her into the hospital, where she was told that the woman could not be admitted. She had no money and she was obviously going to die anyway. There were so many others who could be admitted who might at least be helped by medical attention. The alternative seemed to be to take the woman back outside and let her die on the street.

But Mother Teresa refused to leave. "They only took her in because I refused to move," she recalls. "From there I went to the municipality and I asked them to give me a place where I could bring these people, for on the same day I had found other people dying in the streets."

It was an unusual request, especially coming from a woman who, although she wore a cotton sari, was obviously a foreigner and one, moreover, who spoke English with an accent. But Mother Teresa's work in the slums had been noted by some officials of the Calcutta Corporation, the city's governing body. It was agreed to at least let her look at a "place."

# 5
# Immaculate Heart

The district of Kalighat sprawls on the banks of the brown Hooghly River in south Calcutta. The Kali Temple there is sacred to Hindus, for Kali, "the black one," the consort of Siva, is a powerful goddess and the sacred waters of the Ganges flow through the Hooghly.

Hindus believe that a demon once roamed the earth, devouring man as he was created. Kali killed the demon, but from his drops of blood other demons arose. The goddess then fashioned two men from the perspiration of her arms and commanded them to strangle the demons without shedding any blood. The two men did this and soon all the demons had vanished.

According to a Hindu legend, Kali's father made a sacrifice so that he might have a son but did not include Shiva, Kali's husband, in the ceremony. Kali was so insulted that she killed herself. Her grief-stricken husband carried her body through the world, threatening to destroy it in his madness. But Vishnu saved the world by hurling a discus at Kali's corpse, scattering pieces of it all over the world. The ground was sanctified wherever the pieces fell. The most sanctified place of all was where the toes of Kali's right foot fell, the Kalighat.

Public religious rites are held for Kali every year in Calcutta and devout Hindus wish to go to the Kalighat to die. The Kali Temple, built in a sugar loaf style, rises serenely above narrow, congested lanes, pilgrims' rest houses, and *ghats* where the dead are cremated. Hindus of all castes, rich and poor, come to the temple to place offerings on the black stone statue of Kali, which has a gold tongue hanging to the death goddess' chest. On the night of her feast, the walls of the temple are daubed with the blood of slaughtered buffaloes, goats, and sheep.

Troubadours, peddlers, yogis, beggars, pilgrims, and tourists crowd around the gray walls of the temple, as do *goondas*—loafers and thugs. "The atmosphere of the old market and the neighboring streets, especially in the evening, is rather frightening," counsels Fodor's guide to India.

The Health Officer of the Calcutta Corporation brought Mother Teresa to the Kali Temple and showed her the *dormashalah*. This was a long, low whitewashed building of two rooms once used by Hindu pilgrims as a resting place after they had worshiped Kali. It was now empty, but was sometimes used as a meeting place for thieves, drug addicts, and gamblers. The Health Officer offered the free use of the *dormashalah* to the Missionaries of Charity.

"I was very happy to have that place for many reasons," Mother Teresa remembers, "but especially after learning that it was a center of worship and devotion to the Hindus. Within twenty-four hours we had our patients there and we started the work of the home for the sick and the dying who are destitutes."

It was given the name *Nirmal Hriday*, Immaculate Heart, and was intended as a place where the penniless and dying of the streets could die in some kind of dignity and peace, surrounded by love.

"We help the poor die with God," Mother Teresa

has explained. "It is between them and God alone. Nobody else. Nobody has the right to come in at that time. We just help them to make their peace with God because that is the greatest need—to die in peace with God. We live that they may die, so that they may go home [die] according to what is written in the book, be it written according to the Hindu, or Muslim, or Buddhist, or Catholic, or Protestant, or any other belief."

But this unprecedented act of Christian charity and love was not understood or accepted by many Indians. For one thing, the stench coming from the two rooms filled with the sick and dying was disturbing when it mingled with the already humid, fetid air of Calcutta. More importantly, the rumor got around that the foreign lady was simply using *Nirmal Hriday* as an excuse to convert helpless, lonely Hindus to Christianity before they died.

Stones and brickbats were thrown at Immaculate Heart. The Missionaries of Charity were jostled and threatened with death as they tried to bring in the dying on litters.

But it was never Mother Teresa's purpose to convert the poor to Christianity or, more specifically, to Roman Catholicism. This was hard to believe. Why then engage in this ghastly work which no one else wanted to do?

"Conversion is not our part of the work because only God can convert," Mother Teresa has explained. "Only God can give the grace of faith. But ours is to bring people to come close to each other, to know each other better; and, as Christ has said, 'Love one another as I have loved you.' And by doing that, Christians or non-Christians, they become better and they come closer to God. And once they are face to face with God and the work that they have done, it's for them to accept God in their life or to reject Him. And if they accept, they are converted; and if they reject Him, then it is their own answer."

The records showed then—as they show now—that the vast majority of people comforted at Immaculate Heart were Hindus, followed by Moslems, Buddhists, and Christians, and that if they died and were buried or cremated, it was according to their own religious preference. Neverthless, opposition continued.

"In the beginning we weren't accepted at all," says Mother Teresa. "We had quite a lot of trouble. At one time some young people were going around threatening and destroying and our people were getting more and more frightened. One day I said, 'If this is the way you want it, kill me. I will go straight to Heaven. But you must stop this nonsense.'"

The threats slackened off, but some local youths went to the Police Commissioner and insisted that the foreign lady be put out of Kalighat because she was converting the poor to Christianity. The Police Commissioner gave his word to do this, but said that he would like to examine the situation personally first. He went to Kalighat, entered Immaculate Heart, and found Mother Teresa applying potassium permanganate to the sores of a dying man from which maggots were crawling out. The foreign lady seemed preoccupied, so the Police Commissioner declined her offer to act as guide and walked through the two rooms himself.

When the Commissioner returned he stood over Mother Teresa as she continued to sponge the man's sores. Some local youths then came in; there was nothing to stop them. The Police Commissioner faced the youths and said: "I have given my word that I would push this lady out and I will keep it. But, before I do, you must get your mothers and your sisters to do the work she is doing. Only then will I exercise my authority."

The Police Commissioner did not have to keep his promise. But perhaps the real turning point came when Mother Teresa saw a crowd gathered around a man of about twenty-five crumpled on the pavement outside the Kali Temple. He was lying in a pool of his own filth caused by vomiting and diarrhea. No hospital would take the man and no one in the crowd would go near him. Mother Teresa realized that he was dying of cholera, an acute infectious disease common in humid regions where filth and poor sanitary conditions are prevalent.

Why bother with this dying man? Why also run the gamut of the local youths' hostility? Why not simply return to the convent where peace and a valuable vocation always waited?

Although these were logical questions that might have occurred to Mother Teresa, she nevertheless picked the man up and brought him into *Nirmal Hriday*. At first he was bitter at the fate that had claimed him, but he died in peace after being nursed for two weeks. He had been a priest at the Kali Temple. When the other priests visited him they realized the good that the Missionaries of Charity were doing.

The resentment and protests stopped. Soon Hindu pilgrims on their way to bring offerings to Kali paused to bring small gifts of food to the Missionaries of Charity. The Calcutta Corporation authorized a yearly subsidy of $20,000 for *Nirmal Hriday*.

Since it was opened, more than 33,000 destitute

dying have been brought to *Nirmal Hriday*, Immaculate Heart. About 15,000 of them have died there.

As for those who don't die, Mother Teresa explains: "Those who are able to work we try to find some work for them, the others we try to send them to homes where they can spend at least a few years in happiness and comfort."

At first the Sisters found the dying in the streets and brought them to Immaculate Heart. "But as the work became more and more known," Mother Teresa says, "more and more people came to hear there was a place where these people could be cared for. They telephone for the municipal ambulance and it comes and picks them up and brings them to us. But under one condition, that they have first to take them to the nearest hospital. . . . The home is meant only for the street cases and cases that no hospital wants or for people who have absolutely no one to take care of them."

The work at Immaculate Heart continues today, when it is more needed than ever. There are no doors to the one-story yellow house. A visitor first enters a small reception area, part of the men's ward which occupies the first room. The second room is the women's ward. Each room can accommodate about seventy people. The light is gloomy, with thin shafts of daylight coming through barred windows.

In both rooms are beds jammed together so tightly that it is difficult to move between them. They have narrow metal frames and mattresses sheathed in polyethylene. There are no bedclothes, and the beds are low so that their occupants won't injure themselves if they fall out of them.

Sisters move through the gloom carrying food and bedpans and bandages, pausing to scrape layers of dirt from the face of a new arrival or to hold the stick-like hands of a moaning old woman. Lying or sitting upright in the beds are wrinkled, gaunt, wild-eyed or dumbly staring men and women, some disfigured, some almost naked.

In a corner stands a large pot of steaming rice—often the last meal of the dying. There is a rancid smell that no antiseptic or deodorant can overcome, and occasional whimpers, death rattles, and screams. An adjacent morgue consists of a simple room with cement shelves.

A leaflet about the work of the congregation describes a typical case, a woman who was brought in from a sewer: "She was a beggar who had, apparently overcome by hunger and fatigue, fallen into an open manhole. She lay there for five days barely alive and covered with maggots. As Mother put her to bed and began gently cleaning her, whole areas of skin came off in her hand. The woman, half-conscious, murmured, 'Why are you doing this for me?' Mother replied, 'For the love of God.' This poor waif who probably never in her life had had loving hands tend her—looking at Mother, her soul in her eyes, faith in human nature restored—gave Mother a most beautiful smile and died. That is our reward—that we should make the last moments of the fellow being beautiful."

And it is true that the overall atmosphere of Immaculate Heart is one of a curious peace.

"None of our people have died in distress or in despair," Mother Teresa says. "Most of them have died very beautifully. As one of them said once as we brought him from the street, 'I have lived like an animal in the street but I'm going to die like an angel, loved and cared for.'"

41

The favorite ejaculation of the Sisters of the Missionaries of Charity as they go about their work is: "Immaculate Heart of Mary, cause of our joy, pray for us." And inside the open entrance to the Home for Dying Destitutes a visitor sees a small illuminated glass case. It contains a statue wearing around its waist the ribbon and medal of the Padmashree, the Order of the Lotus. In 1962, Mother Teresa, who became an Indian citizen in 1948, was the first person not of Indian birth to be given this highest civilian award of the Indian government.

The statue wearing the Order of the Lotus is one of the Virgin Mary.

# 6
# A Gift

What would you do if you were approached by a leper crying for alms or begging for help?

This is a question that few Americans will ever have to answer. However, while leprosy has largely been eradicated in the industrialized nations, there are still about twelve million lepers in the underdeveloped world. About three million victims of this slowly progressive mutilating disease try to exist in India.

Leprosy, together with the fear and loathing that it inspires, stretches back into antiquity. Much evidence suggests that the disease was widespread throughout Japan, China, and India at least a thousand years before Christ, although its exact origin is unknown. In the Old Testament, we can read in Leviticus 13, written about 700 B.C.: "The leper in whom the plague is, his clothes shall be rent, and his head bare, and he shall put a covering upon his upper lip, and shall cry, 'Unclean, unclean.' "

The symptoms of what is now defined as leprosy, or Hansen's disease, were first accurately recorded in the *Suskruta Samhitra*, an Indian medical treatise of about 600 B.C. In all places the leper was banished from his community, isolated, and looked upon as an outcast with whom no healthy person would dare to have any contact or communication.

43

This was not the attitude of Christ, however. In Matthew 8 we read: "Jesus put forth His hand, and touched him, saying, 'Be thou clean.' And immediately his leprosy was cleansed."

Leprosy began to appear in Europe about 100 A.D., probably brought from the Middle East by Roman legionnaires or their followers. Returning Crusaders disseminated the disease still farther. By the beginning of the thirteenth century there were at least 2,000 leprosariums in France and perhaps 19,000 in all Europe. No disease aroused such emotional loathing and rejection of the afflicted, causing them to be banished from their homes and deprived of their civil rights.

This extreme reaction was undoubtedly caused by three principal factors. First, there was the fear of contagion. Then there was the continuing mystery surrounding the exact origins of the disease and its mode of transmission (which are today still not fully understood). Were the victims in some strange way being punished for their sins? Finally, there were the hideous visible symptoms. The onset of leprosy is intermittent and gradual and symptoms of the disease may not appear until many years after exposure (it can be arrested now if detected early, but there were no cures in the Middle Ages). Then, as now, symptoms included running sores, missing noses and fingers, stump-like feet, croaking voices, claw hands, and thickening and lining of the skin, giving the face a leonine appearance.

Francesco (Francis) di Bernardone, as a youth, was one of those who shared his contemporaries' horror of lepers. Francis, who would one day found the Franciscans and be canonized as St. Francis of Assisi, claimed that he could smell a leper two miles off, and he would clamp a hand over his nose to ward off their infection.

In the late spring of 1206, Francis returned to Assisi from a pilgrimage to Rome and St. Peter's. The young and once self-indulgent son of a wealthy merchant began to wander alone through the countryside, engaging in self-examination and self-accusation, seeking to determine his relationship to God.

One day he rode on horseback past a leper hospital operated by devout churchmen. Francis saw a leper who had wandered, against the rules, from the hospital and was standing in the road. Francis spurred his horse and rode on. Then, suddenly filled with shame, he rode back, dismounted, and kissed the leper on his drooling mouth.

Centuries later, when questioned about the austerity of the Missionaries of Charity and their work among the poorest of the poor, Mother Teresa would comment: "After all, it was in kissing a leper's hideous sores that St. Francis found the strength to captivate the world and gather around him some of the most audacious spirits of the age, to whom he offered only the glory of being naked on the naked earth for Christ's sake. If the demands had been less, so would the response have been."

In the spring following his encounter with the leper, Francis—after a winter of prayer and soul-searching—took to the roads again in the hills north of Assisi. To subdue his lingering pride, he concluded that he must embrace the world's misery and evil. Their most obvious manifestation were the lepers, so he went to the Lazar House near Assisi and offered his services.

He washed the inmates' rotting feet, bandaged their open sores, and cleansed and even kissed their ghastly wounds.

Francis later wrote in his *Testament*: "When I was still in sin, the mere sight of lepers was unbearable to me. But the Lord himself brought me among them and I tended them with all good will. By the time I left them, what had seemed to me so ugly had turned into sweetness in body and mind. So I waited a little while, and then said farewell to the world."

Francis consecrated his life to the ideal of simplicity and sacrifice and, as *Il Poverello*, the Little Poor Man, begged for alms, devoted himself to others, and practiced Christ's instructions to his apostles as recorded in Matthew 10: "Heal the sick, cleanse lepers, cast out demons. . . . Take no gold, nor silver, nor copper in your belts, no bag for your journey, nor two tunics, nor sandals, nor a staff."

Today, the Missionaries of Charity and their co-workers throughout the world each day say this prayer written by St. Francis of Assisi:

Lord, make me an instrument of Your peace.
Where there is hatred, let me sow love;
Where there is injury, pardon;
Where there is doubt, faith;
Where there is despair, hope;
Where there is darkness, light;
And where there is sadness, joy.

O Divine Master, grant that I may not
So much seek to be consoled as to console;
To be understood as to understand;
To be loved as to love;

For it is in giving that we receive;
It is in pardoning that we are pardoned;
And it is in dying
That we are born to eternal life."

It was in the spirit of this prayer that Mother Teresa and the growing number of Sisters of the Missionaries of Charity began in 1957 a mission that most people would consider dangerous and revolting.

"We started with five lepers who came to our home because they had been thrown out from their work," Mother Teresa remembers. "They could get no shelter; they had to go begging. With them a doctor soon came to help us, and he's still with us, Dr. Senn. He has also been training our Sisters for the leprosy work, because he's a specialist in leprosy work. Among the lepers there are many well-educated people, many rich and capable people. But owing to the disease, they have been thrown out of society, out of their homes, by their relations, and very often even their own children do not want to see them anymore. They get isolated from their own families and have no alternative but to turn to begging. Very often you see people going to the furthest north just to be far away from the people and from the places where they have been known and served and loved. We have among our lepers here in Calcutta very capable people who have had very high positions in life. But owing to the disease, they are now living in the slums, unknown, unloved and uncared for. Thank God our Sisters are there to love them and to be their friends and to bring the rich closer to them."

Article 17 of the Constitution of the Republic of India, which came into force on January 26, 1950, states: "Untouchability is abolished and its practice in

47

any form is forbidden." Although ancient prejudices remained, this legislation alleviated the plight of the untouchables somewhat and they were at last permitted to enter Hindu temples. But nothing, it seemed, could help the lepers. Once having contracted the disease, the victim truly became an outcast, shunned by even the lowliest beggars who shrank away if a leper crawled near them. Lepers were still considered unclean as they had been in biblical times and in medieval Europe. They herded together in the slums or hid away alone under railway bridges or in abandoned factories, scavenging for food in rubbish heaps or begging.

The Indian government and organizations like the Gandhi Memorial Leprosy Foundation and the Ramakrishna Mission offered medical help to those who would accept it, but the basic problem was the same as it was with the starving; the sheer numbers of the afflicted overwhelmed the relief efforts. And although leprosy attacked all classes, the vast majority of the victims were illiterates who often did not seek out medical help or follow it when they did.

Mother Teresa learned that leprosy can be arrested if detected in time and that there are drugs that can relieve the suffering of more advanced cases. She also learned that it is not clearly known how the leprosy bacillus gets into the body, although it appears most likely to be transmitted by the constant contact of hot, humid squalor. Leprosy, however, is not a highly contagious disease, despite the fear of it going back to antiquity. There were, of course, risks of infection in touching lepers, but these were risks the Missionaries of Charity were prepared to take if the lepers were to be helped.

Mother Teresa realized that she did not have the

means to build a hospital where the lepers could come to the Missionaries of Charity for treatment. Therefore she conceived the idea of going out to the leper camps with mobile dispensaries, bringing advice and medicines and—something new—Christian love to the unwanted outcasts. The work of the Missionaries of Charity, which had started with nothing but faith and hope, was increasingly attracting attention and approval. Prime Minister Nehru and the Pope both looked with favor on their work. Food, drugs, money, and land were being provided by the Calcutta Corporation, the Indian government, CARITAS, the Catholic Relief Services, and private individuals, although never enough, it seemed, for the magnitude of the task.

Most of the Sisters were trained in leprosy work, an ambulance and drugs were acquired, and the Sisters went out to the leper camps. One of their first visits was to Titagarh in the industrial suburbs, the site of paper and jute mills and also rows of shanties built on stilts over open drains. Here lepers squatted on unoccupied land owned by the railways running parallel to a busy railway line. And here the Sisters established one of their first centers, bringing medicines, bathing ulcerous sores, teaching simple trades to the afflicted, and even performing minor surgery.

Since the treatment for leprosy is a long one, many victims wander away before it is completed. There are unfortunate accidents. Lepers can't feel pain or heat in their hands or feet and some are badly burned. A few of the blind or maimed stray onto the railway tracks, can't avoid the onrushing trains, and are run over. But, in general, the Sisters' work at Titagarh succeeded. And the work was always done with Christian love for the individual. About five thousand lepers at a time now attend the outdoor clinic, and Christmas Mass is celebrated each year for all those who wish to attend.

More rehabilitation centers followed the one at Titagarh, but Mother Teresa conceived a dream of building a permanent colony for lepers where families could live together in their own homes and be able to develop small crafts and industries. To many this might have seemed an impossible dream, but Mother Teresa has always believed that "God will provide." And the Indian government did donate to the Missionaries of Charity thirty-four acres of land at Shantinagar, a coal-mining area two hundred miles from Calcutta. But where were the large sums of money needed to build homes and a clinic to come from?

Then, in December 1964, Pope Paul VI came to Bombay to attend an International Eucharistic Congress. To help him travel about, the Pope was presented with a huge white Lincoln limousine by some American admirers. He never used it, but rode in a white jeep instead. When the Congress ended, the Pope gave the Lincoln to Mother Teresa. "When he gave that car," she has said, "he said that he was giving the car to Mother Teresa to share in her universal mission of love."

But what would Mother Teresa really do with a white Lincoln limousine in the slums? She promptly raffled it off and raised some $100,000 which she put into building the town for lepers at Shantinagar, which she called The Place of Peace. Nevertheless, the work went slowly and more funds were needed.

Then, on December 6, 1971, Mother Teresa was awarded the Pope John XXIII Peace Prize by Pope Paul VI in the great hall of the Consistorium in the

Vatican. In concluding his remarks while making the award the Pope said:

> Once again in the history of the Church and in society in progress, the Gospel has been accomplished and again the joy of good is lighted, the hope of an ideal life, the luminous truth of the words of Irenaeus: "The glory of God in man fully alive." All this takes on great importance in the modern world which is growing up in the effort at sincerity and understands the enormous needs which have appeared in present-day society on a worldwide scale: ignorance, hunger, sickness, crumbling standards, and the dangers of its own conquests. Man must now make enormous efforts for his fellow man, efforts that powerful and generous undertakings have put in motion; but a need which is called for by these very undertakings is that the human ideal should not grow dim, but that it should always have numerous and new witnesses. . . . She who presents herself as a Missionary of Charity is an apostle of the Brotherhood. That is why we are giving her the Prize for Peace.

The Pope handed to Mother Teresa a check for fifteen million lire (about $22,000) which accompanied the prize and she used it to further the construction at Shantinagar, which is still not completed. However, The Place of Peace does have a tree-lined main road, Pope Paul VI Avenue, small cottages where families live together, vegetable gardens, a poultry farm, pig pens, small wards for seriously afflicted lepers, ponds for raising ducks and geese, a school, and a crèche for children born there.

The Missionaries of Charity now operate sixty-seven leprosariums around the world and care for about 46,000 lepers in all regions of India.

"Now the government of India has been giving us land in many states to be able to rehabilitate our lepers because they are the people who are most shunned and unwanted by anybody," Mother Teresa says. "But, thank God, now there is this new way of rehabilitating them and they are becoming more and more normal and feeling more wanted and loved because they are among their own."

There are some critics who maintain that the work of the Missionaries of Charity with the dying destitutes and the lepers is insignificant and that in view of the size of the problem only a massive collective government program would be of any use. To this, Mother Teresa replies: "I do not agree with the big way of doing things. To us what matters is an individual. To get to love the person we must come in close contact with him. If we wait till we get the numbers, then we will be lost in the numbers. And we will never be able to show that love and respect for the person. I believe in person to person; every person is Christ for me, and since there is only one Jesus, that person is only one person in the world for me at that moment."

Mother Teresa and the Sisters put this philosophy into action daily. In a typical example, two Sisters in white saris can be seen on a summer morning, with the temperature at 117°, walking through Belgachia, a large Calcutta slum and the site of a dumping ground and a sewage center. The Sisters walk along a dirty canal and see a ragged man curled up in an open drain.

52

Crowds bustle past the man, paying him no attention. But—like St. Francis so many centuries ago—the Sisters approach the man and realize that he is a leper.

He cannot move. The muscles of his stick-like legs are paralyzed and his feet are filthy stumps. Flies cluster on the open sores of his face and neck. His vocal cords are so damaged that he cannot tell the Sisters his name, how he got to this open drain, or how old he is. He is, however, an old man and he is obviously dying. Unlike other fatal diseases, leprosy does not often kill quickly. Lepers can linger on for a lifetime. But this man—abandoned, totally ignored by the passers-by— has finally come to the end of decades of suffering.

The Sisters pick him up by the arms—he weighs no more than eighty pounds—and carry him for half a mile in the sweltering heat to the clinic at the leper city built by the Missionaries of Charity in Belgachia. There he is given food and an injection of pain-killing drugs, and he is cleaned. The unknown man revives enough to whisper a request to the Sisters in Bengali—he knows that he is about to die, but before he does he wants his lips to be wet with water from the sacred Ganges. The Sisters go to the nearby Hooghly River, into whose waters the Ganges runs, fill a bottle with water, return and grant the man's request. He dies that afternoon with a slight smile on his gaunt face as the Sisters pray over him and hold his hands. It is probably the only time since he first contracted leprosy decades before that anyone has paid any attention to him as a human being.

The Sisters make arrangements with two young lepers at the camp who are responding to treatment to see to it that the unknown man is given a Hindu burial. That afternoon the Sisters return to Belgachia. In a crowded alley they notice something stirring at the top of an overflowing garbage can. It is a naked baby girl, perhaps a week old.

Again, this sight is ignored by the passers-by. It is not all that uncommon. Indeed, there are those who maintain that, since there are too many poor people in India already, abandoned babies—especially girls—would be better off dead. Why shouldn't the Sisters, too, simply pass by?

# 7
# The Little Children

As the Sisters did not pass by the old leper, they go to the garbage can and pick up the baby. When they do so, two large rats scurry away over their open-toed sandals.

One of the Sisters cradles the emaciated baby in her arms and, with her companion, gets on a trolley car. A taxi, of course, would be faster but they cannot afford a taxi. They ride to a two-storied building not far from Creek Lane and the first house where Mr. Gomes gave Mother Teresa shelter.

There is a high gray wall in front of the building, broken by a green iron gate for vehicles and a small brown door with a bell and chain. On the face of the building behind the wall one can see a large crucifix and under it the words: NIRMALA SHISHU BHAVAN. This is the Missionaries of Charity's Home for Abandoned Children and main work center in Calcutta, opened in 1955.

The Sisters open the door and enter a courtyard that contains the model of a grotto, a statue of the Virgin Mary, and shaded seats for the weary. There are young children playing everywhere.

Next to the main building there is a busy dispensary and a huge kitchen in which nuns are cooking. From this kitchen the long lines of ragged, hungry people waiting patiently outside in the dusty street are fed.

The Sisters take the baby to a room in the main building filled with cribs in which scores of other abandoned infants lie. The little girl is bathed, fed, given medical attention, and dressed. But it is only after a full week in the Sisters' care that she smiles, perhaps for the first time in her life.

Abandoned children like this one are another principal concern of the Missionaries of Charity, and with good reason. India, with 654 million people—a figure growing by a million a month—has fifteen percent of the world's population on only 2.4 percent of its land. Thousands of babies are abandoned every week by their parents, themselves homeless, hungry, and penniless.

The Missionaries of Charity search out these unwanted children and orphans, too, finding them on doorsteps and pavements, under trees, in front of police stations, in marshes, city hospitals, even in jails. They are brought to *Shishu Bhavan*, where many of them die within hours or days. They have contracted incurable diseases or, having been born prematurely or through forced birth, are too tiny and weak to survive. The high death rate does not deter Mother Teresa, who believes that no baby should die unloved and uncared for.

Many others do survive. But does it matter? What of those who say that there are too many people, too many children, in India and that saving a few from death is meaningless and only adds to the population problem?

To this, Mother Teresa replies: "Yes, many would die, especially among those children that are unwanted. Quite possibly they would have been either thrown away or killed. But that way is not for us; our way is to preserve life, the life of Christ in the life of the child. . . . I do not agree because God always provides. He provides for the flowers and the birds, for everything in the world that he has created. And those little children are his life. There can never be enough."

The Missionaries of Charity, overworked as they are, have never refused to take in an abandoned baby or an orphaned older child. They have cared for over three thousand children since opening *Shishu Bhavan*, which can house about one hundred of them at a time. The children range in age from day-old babies to teenage girls who sleep in a separate dormitory. Older boys are sent to a little Boys' Town run by the Catholic Church at Gangarampur.

At *Shishu Bhavan*, the Sisters teach the children and try to find them foster parents. Later, they find them jobs and even arrange marriages and provide small dowries for the girls. It is still difficult in India for a young girl without a dowry to find a husband.

But, as was the case with the Home for Dying Destitutes, Mother Teresa's work did not inspire universal admiration. In arranging for adoptions, she was able to place many of her charges in comfortable homes outside India. Then came accusations that the foreign nuns were stealing and selling Indian children, along with bizarre charges of "nun-running." The government ordered the adoptions outside India halted. It was several years before this restriction was lifted. Now the baby girl found on a Calcutta garbage can might someday find herself living with a family in the United States or Europe.

Sponsorship, rather than outright adoption, is another means developed by the Missionaries of Charity to help the children in their care. Individuals will donate money for a specific child. The Sisters will use the funds to board the child and see him through vocational school, visiting him and encouraging him to correspond with his sponsor.

Christmas is a happy time at *Shishu Bhavan.* There is a crèche and a gaily festooned tree. In the pink decorated rooms, laughing toddlers bounce around or sit on the floor playing with the nuns, clutching a teddy bear or a doll; each child has a present. It is difficult to remember that each of these healthy children would probably be dead if it had not been taken into *Shishu Bhavan.* But would it not really have been better if they had never been born?

"It is not for us to decide," Mother Teresa has said. "Only God can decide life and death. The healthy person may be closer to dying or even more dead than the person who is dying. The healthy person might be spiritually dead, only it doesn't show. Who are we to decide? That is why abortion is such a terrible sin. You are not only killing life, but putting self before God; yet people decide who has to live and who has to die. They want to make themselves Almighty God. They want to take the power of God in their hands. They want to say, 'I can do without God. I can decide.' That is the most devilish thing that a human hand can do. That is why we are paying with such terrible things happening in the world. It is a punishment; it is the cry of those children continually coming before God."

After establishing *Shishu Bhavan* in Calcutta, Mother Teresa opened another Home for Abandoned Children in New Delhi, and others followed. The home in New Delhi was inaugurated by Jawaharlal Nehru. When Mother Teresa requested permission of the Prime Minister to explain to him the work of the Missionaries of Charity, he said: "No, Mother, you need not. I know about it. That's why I'm here."

Although precise figures are hard to come by because they are constantly rising and the Sisters spend much more of their time helping the poor than in keeping records, the Missionaries of Charity presently operate about twenty-eight homes for almost two thousand abandoned children. And the number of Homes for Dying Destitutes throughout India has risen to over thirty, also caring for about two thousand of the unwanted at any given time.

The Missionaries of Charity also operate some eighty schools, with four thousand pupils in Calcutta alone. "They are just little primary schools," Mother Teresa says, "where we teach the children to love the school and be clean and so on. If we didn't have these little schools, those children, those thousands of children, would be left in the street."

In caring for the dying, the lepers, the abandoned children, the Missionaries of Charity always try to bring them not just material help but love. "We must be able to radiate the joy of Christ," Mother Teresa says, "and express it in our actions. If our actions are just useful actions that give no joy to people, our poor people would never be able to rise up to the call which we want them to hear, the call to come closer to God. We want to make them feel that they are loved. If we went to them with a sad face, we would only make them much more depressed."

To Mother Teresa, the worst disease that any human being can experience is being unwanted.

As the work of the Missionaries of Charity grew from the single slum school in *Moti Jheel* and became astonishingly diversified, the danger also grew that the congregation would become so involved in social work that its original purpose of giving the love of Christ would be submerged. That is why the Sisters, no matter what else they are doing, must spend at least part of each day working among the poorest of the poor in the slums. "Here in the slums," Mother Teresa says, "in the broken body, in the children, we see Christ and we touch him."

But does it really mean anything, putting these drops of Christian love and charity into the ocean of misery and despair that is India's slums? Each human being has to answer that question for himself.

However, in Mother Teresa's small office in *Shishu Bhavan* there is an album of photographs of adopted children of all ages. There is one photo of a smiling Indian boy of about ten. He is wearing a cowboy hat and pointing a toy pistol. He now lives somewhere in America, where he was placed for adoption by the Missionaries of Charity.

Had it not been for the Missionaries of Charity, the boy would undoubtedly have died years before in some garbage dump or open drain in Calcutta.

# 8
# The Hunger

The Missionaries of Charity remained in Calcutta for ten years after their congregation received papal approval in 1950. Then the Sisters carried their mission to other parts of India and gradually into the slums of other countries.

In 1963 Mother Teresa began to feel a need for men to care for the boys in the schools run by the Missionaries of Charity, as well as the men in the Home for Dying Destitutes and in the mission on the Kiddepore docks of Calcutta. She recognized that there were some things women could not do for these men, so she asked permission of the Archbishop of Calcutta to found the Missionary Brothers of Charity and it was granted on March 25, 1963.

There were nine Brothers at first. In 1965, they were joined by Father Ian Travers-Ball, a tall, thin Australian Jesuit. As Brother Andrew, he became the first Superior of the Missionary Brothers of Charity. "I think for a long time he was working to give himself totally to the poor," Mother Teresa has said. "He is a very holy person, really very holy. He was a very gifted Jesuit in every possible way—spiritually, mentally, and physically. And both of us have the same mind. That is the most extraordinary thing. But we are so different. Naturally, he is much more gifted than I, very gifted."

There are now over one hundred and seventy-five Missionary Brothers of Charity, a few of them ordained priests. They have eleven communities in India. However, according to Brother Andrew: "We lost five houses in Vietnam and Cambodia. The buildings don't matter. But to be separated so finally from all the people one came to know is unbelievably painful. . . . So, 1975 saw the end of our work in Indochina. But it saw a wonderful deepening of the Brothers' work and spirit in India. . . . Out of the tragedy of Vietnam and Cambodia we now have a beautiful little community of Brothers in Los Angeles working on Skid Row. They had come to be Brothers in Indochina from America and Europe. They are a wonderful group and already penetrate the dark alleys and hotel rooms of the broken men and women swept up, it seems, by a giant broom into the Skid Row of this vast city. . . . Misery and joyful hope, darkness and light, painful sorrow and joy . . . the strange mixture in the lives of us all."

Five Brothers, one Dutchman and four Americans who had served together in South Vietnam and Cambodia, established living quarters in mid-summer 1975 in two tiny rooms with a bath and a kitchen in the impoverished Skid Row area of downtown Los Angeles. Brother Jeremy, an American who is the Servant (Superior) of the Missionary Brothers of Charity in Los Angeles, writes: "Besides our work with the lonely and friendless men on Skid Row, there is always some need in our neighborhood among the poor families. Now the Brothers are working with the street gangs. As usual, it is all developing without us having much to do or say about it. God just seems to drop people right under our noses and shows us what to do. We are so often reminded of Mother Teresa's message that we should 'let

Jesus use us without consulting us.' "

Back in February 1965, the diocesan congregation of the Missionaries of Charity had been made a Society of Pontifical Right, directly responsible to the Pope. This process usually takes many decades longer. "This shows the great love and appreciation the Holy Father has for our work and for the congregation," Mother Teresa says.

In July 1965, the Missionaries of Charity opened their first center outside India in Cocorote, a slum near Caracas, Venezuela. Other centers followed in Colombo, Ceylon in 1967 (closed in 1971); in Tabora, Tanzania, and—at the invitation of the Pope—in a Roman slum, both in 1968; in Bourke, Australia, to help the aborigines, in 1969; Melbourne, Australia, and Amman, Jordan, both in 1970; and Paddington, a London district housing many Indian immigrants, in 1971.

But even as the Missionaries of Charity expanded beyond the borders of India, new troubles were added to the endless old ones on the Indian subcontinent. In 1947, British India had been partitioned into two new nations: predominantly Moslem Pakistan and predominantly Hindu India. Pakistan was something of an artificial creation of two wings—West and East Pakistan—separated by one thousand miles of Indian territory and with no real link between them but the Moslem religion.

The tensions between West Pakistan and East Pakistan erupted on March 25, 1971 into a nine-month guerrilla struggle followed by a thirteen-day war in which the combined forces of East Pakistan and India defeated the Pakistani army. A new state, Bangladesh (the Land of East Bengal), with its capital at Dacca, was established in December 1971 with Indian troops maintaining a form of law and order.

During the struggle, the Pakistani army launched a campaign of terror against the dissident East Bengalis —both Moslems and Hindus—who also suffered at the hands of extreme political fanatics. Ten million refugees fled to India. India's eventual commitment to come to the military aid of what became Bangladesh was, in part, motivated by the prospect of having to care for these refugees over the long-term.

An emergency camp for quarter of a million refugees administered by voluntary international relief agencies was established in a huge swamp outside of Calcutta known as Salt Lake. Teams of Missionaries of Charity went to Salt Lake to comfort the dying and help prevent the outbreak of a cholera epidemic.

In 1971, Mother Teresa received the John F. Kennedy International Humanitarian Award. She used the $20,000 grant that accompanied the award, as well as a personal contribution of $5,000 from Mrs. Joseph Kennedy, to set up the Kennedy Center for Handicapped Children in Dum Dum, near Calcutta. After the Salt Lake camp could be closed, Mother Teresa was able to transfer some of the medical supplies and equipment from it to Dum Dum.

Eventually, most of the ten million refugees returned from India to Bangladesh, one of the poorest countries in the world. Bangladesh has the world's eighth largest population. About eighty million people are jammed into a land about the size of Wisconsin or England and Wales. A third of it is flooded by monsoon rains every year. Malnutrition is almost the norm, and more than half of the population suffers from vitamin and calorie deficiencies.

It is hard to comprehend such figures, but a typical

case is represented by a man we shall call Mr. Abdul Khan. He is a *ricksha-wallah* in the steaming, sprawling capital of Dacca. The *ricksha* is a three-wheeled vehicle or pedicab. The Hindu suffix *wallah* means agent or operator.

Mr. Khan is one of an estimated thirty thousand men who—like beasts of burden—peddle passengers around Dacca for five cents a mile. He earns about thirty dollars a month, but he considers himself fortunate because he can at least buy enough food to survive. He is better off in Dacca than many of the *ricksha-wallahs* in Calcutta who have no cycles to operate and just pull the vehicle along, their bare feet slapping on the pavement. And Mr. Khan is more fortunate than those who try to grow rice—the staple food—on tiny farms in the swampy countryside around Dacca. When the crop fails, thousands starve.

The Missionaries of Charity are doing what they can to help the poorest of the poor in Bangladesh. They have three centers there—at Khulna, Dacca, and Tezgoan, near Dacca. Faced with the staggering immensity of the problem of hunger and poverty in Bangladesh and elsewhere in the underdeveloped world, it would be easy to adopt a cynic's view that the work of the Missionaries of Charity is meaningless. And yet these disciplined, loving women, though relatively few in numbers, find in their work and in one another the fulfillment of life and continue to go out and give the love of Christ.

In 1972, they opened a center to care for poverty-stricken refugees in the heat and dust of the Gaza strip in Israel. Sister Damien now heads a group of seven young Sisters there. They use an ambulance-van for their daily round of service but have to practice restraint—a gallon of gasoline costs almost three dollars in Gaza.

In 1973, more centers were opened in Katherine in the Northern Territories of Australia, in Addis Ababa, Ethiopia, in Lima, Peru, and in Hodeida, Yemen. The Sisters always enter a country by invitation and with the approval of local authorities. They and the priest assigned to them were the first Christians to enter the Arab country of Yemen in eight hundred years. Other centers followed in Palermo, Italy, and Papua, New Guinea, in 1974.

In 1975 the Missionaries of Charity built a second home on the outskirts of Amman, Jordan, to which they could bring the most neglected and abandoned people from the parched east bank near the Jordan River. Their chapel nearby is in a converted chicken coop. Since the chapel has no electricity, the Sisters celebrate Mass by the light of lanterns.

In 1976 they opened a house to serve slum areas in Mexico City. After a devastating earthquake struck Guatemala on February 4, 1976, they opened a house there—the ninety-ninth foundation of the Missionaries of Charity—to aid the victims.

Mother Teresa started out alone, with nothing but her faith, in Calcutta in 1948. There are now over 1,200 Missionaries of Charity aiding the poorest of the poor in sixty-seven different countries.

But there was one place where the work of the Missionaries of Charity was not entirely welcomed. Ironically, it was on the island where Mother Teresa had begun her vocation in the Loretto convent near Dublin. The Missionaries of Charity opened a center in Belfast in October 1971. But there was criticism from both Protestants and Catholics that the Sisters were not adequately trained for their work and that their presence in Belfast was a reflection on the religious communities already serving there. Without any explanation from Mother Teresa or the hierarchy, the Belfast center was closed in 1973.

But elsewhere the Missionaries of Charity have been welcomed and the number of Sisters and Brothers grows steadily. This is happening at a time when the number of priests and nuns in the Catholic Church is dwindling. When asked to account for this paradox, Mother Teresa has said: "I think the youth of today want to give all to Jesus, all or nothing, because in their applications they always put one sentence, which is so very real of the young people of today: 'I want a life of poverty, of prayer and sacrifice that will lead me to the service of the poor.'

"Because our lives are very much woven with the Eucharist, we begin the day with Mass and Holy Communion, and then throughout the day we try to pray the work by doing it *with* Jesus, *for* Jesus and *to* Jesus. And at the end of the day, from half past six to half past seven, we have an hour of adoration; we expose the Blessed Sacrament; we have this full hour of adoration. And also we live a very close community life. And for us poverty is necessary because to be able to understand the poor we must know what is poverty; only our poverty is of choice—we choose.

"And this life of prayer and sacrifice and complete surrender of ourselves to God and to our poor, I think, has made a tremendous demand on the young and they want that. And God has blessed us with many, many vocations. For example, at present [August 1976] we have thirty-five novices in Rome itself, and among them there are sixteen different nationalities. And in

Calcutta we have two hundred and thirty-nine novices."

The work of the Missionaries of Charity is supported by more than 80,000 Co-Workers around the world. The International Association of Co-Workers of Mother Teresa received the blessing of Pope Paul VI in March 1969. This group of volunteers has a constitution whose first paragraph reads that it "consists of men, women, young people and children of all religions and denominations throughout the world who seek to love God in their fellow men, through wholehearted free service to the poorest of the poor of all castes and creeds, and who wish to unite themselves in a spirit of prayer and sacrifice with the work of Mother Teresa and the Missionaries of Charity."

Part of the Co-Workers consists of people who, because of age or infirmity, are unable to offer physical help. They adopt a Sister or Brother. "That person," says Mother Teresa, "offers all her suffering, all prayers, all the pain for that Sister or that Brother. And that Sister or Brother offers everything, all the work and prayers, for the suffering one. So they become second-selves to each other."

A third group consists of members of a contemplative community who adopt one of the communities of the Missionaries of Charity. "We have become like a new life for them," says Mother Teresa, "and they have become a new strength for us. And in all this, among those 80,000 people, there's a tremendous family spirit and a wonderful love and understanding. It doesn't matter to what part of the world you go; wherever there are co-workers, you are at home with them."

As the work of the Missionaries of Charity became known throughout the world, it was recognized by the bestowing of many awards upon Mother Teresa. In addition to India's Order of the Lotus and the Pope John XXIII Peace Prize, she has received (1962) the Magsaysay Award for International Understanding, established to honor the late President of the Philippines, which brought with it a grant of $20,000 which she used for a children's home; the Jawaharlal Nehru Award for International Understanding (1972); the Templeton Award for "Progress in Religion," presented by Prince Philip in 1973 (this award carried with it a gift of $85,000, which Mother Teresa used to further her work); and the "Mater et Magistra" Award, the Third Order of Saint Francis of Assisi (1974).

In 1975, Mother Teresa was given the Ceres Medal by the Food and Agriculture Organization of the United Nations. One side of this medal bears the sculptured image of Mother Teresa. On the other side is the image of a starving child being reached for by two arms. The Ceres Medal is usually awarded to a distinguished scientist who has somehow improved agricultural techniques and production. When asked why she thought she had been an exception, Mother Teresa said: "I think that I myself don't understand why, but I believe that in giving it to me actually they are showing they are concerned that the presence of the poor is being felt. And in giving it to me they're giving it to them. And they are choosing me for that medal, I think, because we are so involved with feeding the hungry."

Mother Teresa was among the candidates under serious consideration for the 1976 Nobel Peace Prize but the Nobel Committee decided not to award the prize that year. She has been awarded honorary degrees by such institutions as Catholic University in Washington, D.C., Holy Cross, and Iona. During an extended trip to the United States in 1976 she came to New Rochelle, N.Y. in the spring to accept the degree of Doctor of Humane Letters, *honoris causa*, from Iona College. Sitting on the podium in her cotton sari with hands clasped in her lap, she provided a startling physical contrast to another recipient, Thomas A. Murphy, Chairman of the Board of General Motors.

Iona's citation for the honorary degree read, in part: "At a time when many in our society question the value of human life as well as permanent commitment in any kind of relationship, Mother Teresa's life of total dedication to serving Christ in the poorest of the poor presents both a challenge and an inspiration. . . . Mother Teresa, and those she has inspired, see Christ in the poor and abandoned and bring to them a sense of personal worth, a feeling of being loved and cared for. To the destitute, the sick, the lonely, the orphaned and abandoned, Mother Teresa symbolizes hope and love. By a joyful and loving service to the individual in need, Mother Teresa seeks to restore a sense of human dignity to those who are outcasts of society."

Three girl students from Iona went to Calcutta that summer to spend their vacations helping the Missionaries of Charity, which probably pleased Mother Teresa more than the honorary degree. She found the time to go to Boys' Town, Nebraska, on May 3 to receive the second Father Flanagan Award for Service to Youth. According to the Director, Father Robert Hupp, "Of all the distinguished visitors to Boys' Town none made a more profound impression on our boys than Mother Teresa. . . . I'll never forget her advice: 'The boys do not need pity, but love and compassion. Give your hands to serve them and your hearts to love them.' "

That summer of 1976 two Boys' Town students, Joe Pearson and Shawn Ellis, both 17, went to India and served with the Missionaries of Charity for one and a half months. They worked with the Sisters and Brothers in slum schools, in the Home for Dying Destitutes, in a jungle village thirty miles outside Calcutta where the Brothers supervised the building of roads and a school house, and in leper colonies.

Upon his return in September, Joe Pearson said: "I found it really fascinating. Lepers are usually withdrawn from society. But these made their own bandages, the women made their own saris, and they made their sandals out of tires. They all worked together."

Both boys were struck by how poor most of Calcutta's residents were, sleeping on the streets or under tents. The boys shared the sparse diet of the Missionaries of Charity and, since it did not include meat, found themselves dreaming of hamburgers and french fries. They were both glad to come back to America, although they said they would return to India if given another opportunity.

That same summer, Mother Teresa visited the headquarters of the Catholic Medical Mission Board in New York City. The Missionaries of Charity depend upon donations and Mother Teresa thanked Father Joseph J. Walter, S.J., Director of the CMMB, for its help. The Missionaries of Charity are only one of numerous Catholic missionary orders in eighty-five countries who regularly receive medical supplies from donors to the CMMB.

"Our shipments to India, totaling more than $7 millions from June 1970 to June 1976, have been gratefully received by our Medical Missionaries laboring in that vast land," according to Father Walter. "Doing whatever they can to help the poor, they are ever thankful for our donors' love and concern."

"We need you, but you also need us," Mother Teresa said during her visit to the CMMB offices. She meant that the Missionaries of Charity depended on the CMMB and its donors for medicines and medical help, but that they also need the Sisters as the instruments of their charity.

In traveling around the world to such organizations as the Catholic Medical Mission Board and in accepting awards and honorary degrees, Mother Teresa, who seeks and wants no personal publicity, makes it plain that she is doing so on behalf of the work of the Missionaries of Charity. Calcutta remains the center of their mission and Mother Teresa works just as hard as she did during the first years in the *Moti Jheel*, begrudging any time spent away from serving the poorest of the poor.

However, at the beginning of August 1976, Mother Teresa came to Philadelphia to attend the 41st International Eucharistic Congress of the Roman Catholic Church. More than a million Christian pilgrims poured into Philadelphia for the congress, whose theme was "The Hungers of the Human Family." For eight days, studies focused on the hunger for God, bread, justice, the Spirit, truth, understanding, peace, and Christ. The first of the hungers was defined in these terms by the official directory of the congress: "That there is a worldwide hunger for meaning today goes without question. Such answers as astrology and neo- or pseudo-Eastern religions are merely the most sensational evidence of a worldwide hunger for God."

But nutrition was placed high on the agenda, emphasizing its growing seriousness as a Church issue. On the first full day of the congress, August 2, a symposium on hunger was held in the Civic Center auditorium. Shortly after noon, a tiny figure in a white sari with blue borders entered the hall, gripping the audience of 6,000 people. Mother Teresa opened the symposium by saying a prayer over a table on which were placed long loaves of round bread. Then she broke one of the loaves and shared its pieces with others.

Among those who then addressed the hunger conference were Archbishop Helder Camara of Olinda and Recife in the poor northeast region of Brazil and the Very Reverend Pedro Arrupe, S.J., Superior General of the Jesuits. Dom Helder Camara broke off his address, saying that he would pause "to kiss the two hands of Mother Teresa," who was sitting nearby. Taking her two gnarled hands in his own, he kissed them reverently and then bestowed upon her the traditional Latin "abrazo."

Father Arrupe outlined the complexities of the hunger problem. Then he proposed one response to it, suggesting that more Christians follow the example of those participating in Operation Rice Bowl. They fasted at least one meal a week and donated the money saved to the Church. Father Arrupe observed: "If this challenge were taken up merely by Roman Catholics and in the United States alone, and if the amount saved only averaged out at $1 per person per week, this would reach the huge sum of over $2.5 billion a year."

As he spoke, a freighter at a Philadelphia pier was being loaded with two thousand tons of rice destined for Bangladesh. It was a gift from contributors in the Philadelphia area to Operation Rice Bowl.

The presence of Mother Teresa at the congress also focused attention on the problem of world hunger and seemed to be a source of inspiration to many who attended. A report in *The New York Times* noted: "Mother Teresa has become the most magnetic figure at the congress. Wherever she goes, crowds follow her, hoping to touch her clothing or to hear her speak."

In order to add further emphasis to the Church's concern for the hungry of the world, the U.S. Catholic Conference arranged for Mother Teresa to be heard by a nationwide television audience. On August 1, the opening day of the Eucharistic Congress, she took part in an hour-long dialogue on NBC-TV with Philip Scharper, editor of Maryknoll's Orbis Books. This dialogue afforded millions a chance to hear Mother Teresa, most undoubtedly for the first time, and to learn something about her work.

Mother Teresa agreed with the main theme of the congress and said: "I think that more and more people are really hungry for God. And to satisfy this hunger for God and for the love of God, Jesus made Himself a bread of life. And to satisfy this human hunger for God, to satisfy our longing for God, we have to feed that hunger by receiving Him in the Holy Eucharist."

As for the criticism that the Missionaries of Charity are simply social workers, and that the state can provide people to do the same things, Mother Teresa commented: "The state can provide many things—except tender love and care. And not only that. We are not social workers; we may be doing social work but we are not social workers because we are really trying to be contemplatives right in the heart of the world and because we take Christ at His word. He said, 'You did it to Me.' And so we are touching Him twenty-four hours."

Another criticism of the Missionaries of Charity is

that—considering the millions of India's homeless, starving poor—their help is only a drop in the bucket. To this, Mother Teresa replied: "It's worth one at a time. Because that one is my brother, my sister. Because the same loving hand of God has created her or him. And so we belong to each other. And even the amount of work we are doing, I still feel, is only a drop in the ocean. But I think if we didn't put that drop in that ocean of suffering, that ocean would be one drop less. And that's what the people are doing in the United States and around the world. I think that if each of us were to put that little drop in the ocean, we would be able to overcome the poverty of the world."

Mother Teresa thanked the Catholic Relief Services for its support in providing funds and food for the Missionaries of Charity to distribute during the past twenty-two years. She said: "They have been, through Bishop Swanstrom, tremendously helpful in sharing, in the feeding and clothing and medical part of our people. And I'm very glad to have this opportunity to thank Bishop Swanstrom and all the people in the United States for having shared their love and their greatness with our people, because out of those thousands of people that we have picked up from the streets, hungry and naked and so on, more than half have been able to be saved because of this generous sharing of people of America with our people."

Mother Teresa was asked why, instead of dealing with the victims of systems of injustice, the Sisters and Brothers didn't attempt to change the political or economic systems that caused the injustice. "Well, for us," she observed, "it's not a waste of time nor life to spend that time just feeding the person today. The work of tomorrow? There are many people who can do that, who can remove the works of injustice and so on. But for us that person needs a shelter now. I think our part is fulfilled there. And by doing our part many people are getting concerned to do the second part—to improve and to help the people, to remove that poverty and that hunger and that nakedness. And that is what I believe —that the hunger of man is being satisfied, the hunger of the rich to share with others, to give to others, and the hunger of the people to come to understand each other, to share with them. Because I feel also that by loving and serving the poor, we are receiving much more from them than we can give to them."

Philip Scharper observed that many people in the United States, where the poor are often invisible, assume that they don't exist because they aren't seen or encountered. To this observation, Mother Teresa replied: "Maybe in the United States we don't see the hungry and the naked and the homeless in the streets. But I think there's much greater poverty, and that is a very spiritual poverty. . . . I believe it is easier to relieve a material poverty. A person who is hungry for a piece of bread or for a plate of rice, by giving that you have already solved the difficulty. But, I think, the people who are hurt, who are lonely, who are unwanted, who are helpless, who are hopeless, who are those like the alcoholics and the people who have forgotten how to smile, who have forgotten what is human love and human touch—I think that is very very great poverty."

Mother Teresa was asked for her evaluation of the American people, and she said: "I think they are a very great people, but sometimes they are a misled people. And I think if they would deepen their love and their understanding for each other, and if they would be more open to the people outside, to share with them more of what they have received—I think that will make them a holy people. Because holiness is not a luxury of the few; it's a simple duty for each of us."

How well have the American people, including American Catholics, as citizens of the world's most favored and richest nation, responded to the pressing needs of those in less fortunate lands? How well have Americans responded to Mother Teresa's call to "share with them more of what they have received"?

It is well known that billions of tax dollars of the American people, channeled through agencies of their government, have gone to aid the underdeveloped countries of the free world. Less well known is the fact that individual American Catholics, through the private agencies of their Church, have tried and are continuing to try to respond to appeals like that of Mother Teresa "to share."

There are many who contend that private charity cannot come to much compared to massive government welfare assistance. But one could also contend that compassion should not be delegated entirely to government, for then Americans would lose an essential element of their humanity and spirituality—the quality of personally caring.

In the link between Mother Teresa and American Catholics one can see that that quality has not been entirely lost, for her appearance at the Eucharistic Congress in Philadelphia was by no means Mother Teresa's first encounter with America and its people.

# 9
# The Sharing

Mother Teresa's first trip outside of India since she began her novitiate there in 1929 was to the United States. The trip took place in October 1960 and was to, of all places, Las Vegas, Nevada.

She was invited by the Foreign Relief Committee of the National Council of Catholic Women to address their thirtieth annual convention. Almost from the beginning, one of the principal supports of the work of the Missionaries of Charity has been the arm of mercy of the bishops of the United States, Catholic Relief Services. In addition, and in cooperation with Catholic Relief Services, the NCCW established its own channel for overseas aid in special programs that expressed the compassion of women's nature.

Mother Teresa agreed to journey to Las Vegas to explain the work of the Missionaries of Charity to the convention delegates and to thank them for their aid. She has always been extremely grateful for the help of the people of the United States through the Catholic relief organizations, calling it "divine providence."

Dressed in rough leather sandals and a cotton sari, the frail figure of Mother Teresa must have been an odd sight among the gambling casinos and bright lights of Las Vegas, but she made a strong impression on the delegates.

"In all her talks with the delegates, Mother Teresa opened the window on world needs far wider than it had ever been before," recalls Eileen Egan of Catholic Relief Services, in *The Works of Peace*: "If any of the delegates had had the slightest temptation to accept uncritically a materialist or pleasure-oriented view of life, divorced from sacrifice and the works of mercy, Mother Teresa's words buttressed their higher nature."

Before addressing the delegates, Mother Teresa was driven out to the desert where she could compose her words and contemplate. She sat near a cactus plant, and before leaving she twined a crown of thorns from some of the long cactus spines. She took it with her when she returned to India and placed the crown on the head of the crucified Christ hanging in the austere chapel of her order's novitiate. It was her only physical souvenir from Las Vegas.

From Las Vegas, Mother Teresa traveled to Peoria, Illinois, in the flat midwest corn belt to thank the Catholic women of that diocese for their help. Since 1958 they had collected funds for the six Mother and Child clinics established by Mother Teresa in Calcutta. Probably the first aid in overseas funds that reached her was a Madonna Plan grant from the Peoria Diocese.

From Peoria, Mother Teresa was driven to Chicago on a road surrounded by golden corn fields and storage bins filled with grain. The car paused before a cluster of twenty storage bins. Mother Teresa surveyed this scene of the earth's rich bounty and said to Eileen Egan, who was accompanying her: "May God bless you for what you are doing for our poor, our mothers, our children, our sick and dying, our lepers. I am glad I came here to see this sight and to meet the good people."

After stopping in Chicago, Mother Teresa flew to New York City with Eileen Egan. Her purpose was to thank Mother Dengal, foundress of the Medical Mission Sisters, who operate hospitals and clinics in India, Pakistan, Africa, Latin America and the United States. The Medical Mission Sisters' help to Mother Teresa dates back to 1948 when she first left the Loretto convent to begin her work. As Eileen Egan puts it:

Mother Teresa had often mentioned to me her gratitude to an American, Mother Anna Dengal, and to the Medical Mission Sisters of Philadelphia. Shortly after she had obtained permission to leave a strictly confined teaching order in Calcutta, she had been invited to live with the Medical Mission Sisters at Patna, some two hundred miles away.

At their Patna Holy Family Hospital, the Sisters brought to Indian women their skills as nurses, laboratory experts and doctors. In her months as their guest, Mother Teresa received a course in practical nursing, a brief, immensely valuable experience for a woman who was to take on the burdens of the destitute and dying in a refugee-swollen city.

When she prepared to leave Patna, Mother Teresa was already enveloped in the cotton sari of India. The American Sisters as their parting gift gave her a sturdy pair of sandals. These came to be known as the "Patna sandals," since they were passed on to other members of the Missionaries of Charity.

After the meeting in New York between two of the most notable Mother Foundresses of the twentieth century, one possessing the highest medical skills and the other possessing no special skills at all but always desiring to put love into action, Mother Teresa flew to London and the continent before returning to Calcutta. In London, she was able to obtain supplies of an anti-leprosy medicine produced by Imperial Chemical Industries through the help of the Oxford Famine Relief Committee. During a two-week stay on the continent she was able to visit many Catholic relief organizations through the help of the Geneva Office of Catholic Relief Services. More than half a million dollars was pledged so that she could continue her work among the poorest of the poor in India.

The personal visit of Mother Teresa to the United States in 1960 aroused widespread interest in her work, and more aid followed it. For one example, the Brooklyn Diocesan Council of Catholic Women sponsored the entire program when a team of Indian Missionaries of Charity journeyed for the first time to the New World. They worked among the impoverished descendants of African slaves in the State of Yaracuy in Venezuela. American Catholic women have been among Mother Teresa's longest and strongest supporters in providing powdered milk, surplus food, clothing, equipment like mobile vans, and medicines for the Mother and Child clinics all over the world.

But channeling funds through their relief organizations has not been the only way in which American Catholics have responded to the appeal of Mother Teresa. As already noted, the International Association of Co-Workers of Mother Teresa was given the blessing of Pope Paul VI in March 1969. An American branch was formed in December 1971. What exactly is a Co-Worker? A brochure published by the American branch answers the question in this way:

A Co-Worker of Mother Teresa is one who chooses a particular way of life that calls for seeing God in every human being. Seeing God in everyone, starting with those closest to us, often calls for a tremendous change, a transformation, and this transformation brings its fruits. We become ready to share ourselves and our possessions with the lonely, the ill, the poor and the unwanted. We learn the immeasurable power of suffering willingly accepted, of forgiveness freely given, and we are strengthened by being part of a worldwide company of those who bear witness to the presence of God in every member of the family of man. Anyone, of any spiritual tradition, who sees and serves his fellow man in this light may become a Co-Worker.

Anyone interested in becoming a Co-Worker can write to the Chairman of the American branch, Mrs. Warren L. Kump, 4243 Glenwood Avenue, Minneapolis, Minnesota, 55422. The Chairman sends each Co-Worker a Newsletter, from which the description of typical activities that follows is drawn, three times a year.

Co-Workers are active in many diverse ways throughout the United States and keep in touch with each other through their Newsletter. According to Sister Mary Hotard, C.S.J., Vice-Chairman of the Co-Workers in the New Orleans area, they welcomed about sixty Vietnamese families in the fall of 1975.

"We have been conducting a Summer School Program for the children who now number about 200," Sister Hotard writes in the Newsletter. "It has been a joy to share in this work. I feel that we have succeeded in helping the children adjust to their new world, to learn English, and to teach us much about the beauty of their people and their culture. It is very easy to see the face of Jesus in the faces of these children. Please pray for us that we may serve them adequately."

The Co-Workers got started in Alabama after Mrs. Betty Ann O'Brien, Vice Chairman, met Mother Teresa in New York City in 1974. "The meeting with Mother Teresa was a moment of grace," writes Mrs. O'Brien, "and I arrived home in Birmingham knowing that somehow the Co-Workers' formation in Alabama was aborning. . . . In addition to the work with the mentally handicapped, Co-Workers make regular visits to nursing homes, sew clothes for newborn babies, and make simple cloth animals for handicapped and bedridden children at a home in Montgomery, Alabama. Our friends in the nursing home help stuff these animals, and this makes them feel needed. We collect clothing and household articles for the Catholic Center of Concern in Birmingham and a Thrift Shop in Russellville. Several Co-Workers have learned sign language so that they can communicate with the deaf people we visit."

Sister Alicia Panger, O.S.B., vice Chairman, tells of the activities of the Co-Workers in Duluth, Minnesota: "Our meetings are simple. We share and discuss new contacts, listen to Mother Teresa's tapes, and breathe deeply of Jesus' presence in our hour of silent prayer in the Bishop's chapel. Letting Jesus work through us, the Co-Workers each seem to have taken on a way of life suitable to his or her own age level and pattern of living. Younger members visit the aged in rest homes or neighborhoods, playing cards, setting hair, shopping or just chatting. Retired members with cars go to nursing homes or private dwellings every week bringing cheer, goodies, flowers, a smile or a big 'bear hug.' Some have 'adopted' aged friends who haven't a soul to claim, taking them for rides along Lake Superior, remembering their birthdays, calling them on the phone. Older members make layettes for the unwanted babies brought to Mother Teresa. Still others have reached out to alcoholics, the mentally handicapped, disabled or blind to read, or just to be there to listen and care."

The activities of the Co-Workers spread to Texas in 1976. "It was the first Saturday in April, 1976," writes Mrs. Charles W. Plunkett, Vice-Chairman, Texas. "The persons walking into Holy Rosary Church, Houston, Texas, numbered fewer than the Lord's chosen twelve. But they knew Jesus' promise to be with even two gathered in His name, and these had come to pray that the Lord would make them worthy to serve their fellow men throughout the world who live and die in poverty and hunger.

"There was a middle-aged couple who did a lot of 'visiting' through the Legion of Mary and the St. Vincent de Paul Society, a retired nurse now devoting much time to a women's halfway house, a crippled lady on crutches who lives in a low-income government housing project and who spreads joy wherever she goes, and a young Mexican-American man who, with the middle-aged lady, had been concerned about imprisoned men and who takes part in a Mass-confession-visitation program in a large county jail.

"These were the first Co-Workers of Mother Teresa coming together in Houston for a monthly hour of prayer. The newly-named Vice-Chairman had invited them (and they eagerly agreed) to attend the 8 o'clock Mass in the Dominican church on the first Saturday of each month, and then to stay for an hour of private prayer.

"After Mass and the hour of prayer came the 'time of sharing.' This was held under a tree in the church parking lot. The people discussed what they understood a Co-Worker of Mother Teresa should be and encouraged one another to pray that each would serve his fellow man as if that person was Jesus Himself. . . .

"Others have joined the first 'members' in the monthly hour of prayer. Thus, a beginning has been made in Houston to bring together those interested in praying and working more closely with Mother Teresa of Calcutta and her Sisters, Brothers, and Co-Workers all over the world in their work among and devotion to God's neediest."

These are small acts, small gestures of charity, perhaps, but to Mother Teresa they are valuable and important. As she herself put it in a message to the Co-Workers in the spring of 1976:

No Co-Worker, no Missionary of Charity, must drift away from the humble works, because these are the works nobody will do. It is never too small. We are so small that we look at things in a small way. But God, being Almighty, sees everything great, even if you write a letter for a blind man, or you just go and sit and listen, or you take the mail for him, or you visit somebody or bring a flower to somebody, small things, or wash clothes for somebody or clean the house. Both the Brothers and the Sisters, we are determined to remain with the humble works of love.

Very humble work, that is where you and I must be. For there are many people who can do the big things. But there are very few people who will do the small things. It is the small things the Sisters and Brothers do. We can do very little for the people, but at least they know that we love them and that we care for them and that we are at their disposal. It must be the same for the Co-Workers. So let us try, all of us, to come closer to that unity of spreading Christ's love wherever we go. Love and compassion; have deep compassion for the people. People are suffering much: mentally, physically, in every possible way. So you are the ones to bring that hope, that love, that kindness.

Do you want to do something beautiful for God? There is a person who needs you. This is your chance.

In addition to the Co-Workers there is also an American branch of the Sick and Suffering Co-Workers. They are people who wish to become Co-Workers but, because of illness, are not able to take an active part. Instead, they become close Co-Workers of an individual Sister or Brother of the Missionaries of Charity by offering prayers and suffering for and with that Sister or Brother.

Brother Nicholas, O.C.S.O. heads the American branch of Sick and Suffering Co-Workers. Brother

Nicholas is an old friend of Brother Andrew and has been a key link in the foundation of the Missionary Brothers of Charity community in the United States. (Letters about or by Sick and Suffering Co-Workers may be sent direct to Brother Nicholas at Holy Trinity Abbey, Huntsville, Utah, 84317.)

Mother Teresa's gratitude to the Co-Workers, the National Council of Catholic Women, and Catholic Relief Services has been expressed not only by words but—characteristically—by action. As we have seen, the Missionary Brothers of Charity opened a small center in the Skid Row area of Los Angeles in mid-summer 1975 after political events forced them to leave Indochina. But what of the Sisters? They have a definite mission in India, but do they have any place in the richest country in the world?

"India has been receiving; it is time to give, although in a small way," Mother Teresa has said. So she accepted an invitation to establish a convent of the Missionaries of Charity in the United States. It is in the southern half of the Bronx, one of the five boroughs that make up New York City.

Mother Teresa has said. "Maybe in the United States we don't see the hungry and the naked and the homeless in the street." Unfortunately, material poverty, along with spiritual poverty, does exist in the United States. Nowhere is it worse than in the South Bronx. This is a ghetto, a *barrio*, a slum where 350,000 people try to exist. Most of them try to lead decent lives and do so against overwhelming odds and few evidences of love and Christian charity.

But the South Bronx is also a place where many elderly people are prisoners in a world of fear and poverty, existing in small apartments that resemble catacombs for the not-quite-living. The South Bronx is a place where an entire ward of a new health care facility, Lincoln Hospital, is taken over by sixty members of a drug rehabilitation program protesting the lack of inpatient care for addicts. In the South Bronx, a nineteen-year-old member of the Savage Skulls gang is sentenced in November 1976 to twenty-five years to life in prison. He had ordered the torture and execution of a man who had testified against him in a robbery trial. The man, who was retarded, was strangled after his fingernails were pulled out with pliers. Then his body was set on fire. The police precinct serving this area of the South Bronx is known to its officers as Fort Apache. It is here that the Missionaries of Charity try to give the love of Christ.

# 10
# Mission to the South Bronx

The 41st Precinct serving the South Bronx is the most violent in New York City. The "Four-One," as the police call it, was named Fort Apache because the station house was so often besieged by angry mobs wielding chains, knives, and clubs. The police assigned there often feel like a beleaguered band surrounded by hostiles. There is little rapport between them and the community.

The only convent of the Missionaries of Charity in the United States is located in the South Bronx. This is, officially, the 21st Congressional District. It is about a mile from the fashionable Upper East Side of Manhattan, but it is really light years away. Half a million people try to exist in the South Bronx. Forty-four percent of them are Puerto Ricans and forty-three percent are black. Forty-three percent of the residents are under eighteen, often living in large families without fathers.

The South Bronx was once a working-class Italian and Jewish area. Since World War II it has become a metaphor for the decay that afflicts America's inner cities and the poverty that tarnishes the American dream. The unemployment rate is staggering and the South Bronx has the lowest voter turnout of any congressional district in the United States. Except for the aged Jews and Italians who remain largely because they are too poor to move, few people have any roots in the South Bronx and there are few traditional institutions to help with its problems.

Much of the South Bronx is a grim landscape of crowded tenements and abandoned or burnt-out buildings crawling with junkies and rats. Garbage is everywhere—in the gutters, on sidewalks, in lots. There are *bodegas* with *cuchifritos* drying in the windows, tawdry pizza parlors and brightly-lit prostitute bars. Often they serve as fronts for bookies and pushers.

Unlike Calcutta, no one dies of starvation or leprosy in the South Bronx. Decent people try to survive there, but it is a no-man's-land riddled with grief, anger, despair and loneliness, feelings which often erupt into violence and crime. Few people walk on the side streets of the South Bronx after dark.

The young are damaged the most. The Community Service Society estimates that there are fifteen thousand young runaways in New York City. Thousands of them live in the abandoned buildings which exist all over the South Bronx. At night they sleep with newspapers for sheets. During the day they "hang around" and "get high," form gangs, listen to music from transistor radios, fight, beg, and steal.

Sister Lorraine Reilly is a Roman Catholic nun who runs four shelters in the Bronx. One of them is the Group Live-In Experience in the South Bronx, an agency financed by New York City. Here the young are given an opportunity to develop along normal lines. They receive love and discipline and are helped by trained social workers. The runaways come from backgrounds that include drugs, alcohol, brutal beatings by parents, lack of work and lack of any kind of incentive.

"The runaway is often the healthiest person in the

family," Sister Lorraine observes. "Wait till you meet the families. The child who runs away is saying, 'I'm not going to be part of this.' "

Many youngsters can find no hope in the school system. The Board of Education of New York City lists 90,000 youngsters as long-term absentees. They are often referred to as "ghosts." Instead of going to school, they spend aimless hours in the Bronx Zoo, Central Park, or riding the subways. Thousands of these urban nomads create turmoil in the hallways of other schools in the South Bronx, shoplift in stores, and vandalize cars parked outside Yankee Stadium. Late at night they use spray cans to paint on subway cars colorful graffiti and the names of their gangs—"Ghetto Stompers," "Vigilantes," "Conquistadores."

As the young are trapped by hopelessness in the South Bronx, so are the very old. About two years ago violent crimes against old men and women began to escalate rapidly. The South Bronx is not an inviting place in which to grow old. That is especially true if your friends are dead, your children have moved away, you are unable to move away yourself, and you find yourself alone in the world. About a quarter of a million people over sixty try to live in dignity on Social Security or pension checks. But they are being mugged on the streets or in their apartments and sometimes killed.

In response to these increasing attacks, in November 1974 the Police Department set up the Senior Citizens Robbery Unit in the Bronx, the first of its kind in the United States. This unit of sixteen men is led by Sergeant James Bolte out of the 48th Precinct on the Cross-Bronx Expressway. Most of those preying on the elderly are teenagers, with some as young as eleven. Youths under sixteen are not yet subject to adult-criminal laws. Knowing this, they act with boldness and brutality and there are many repeat offenders. The aged are usually frail and unable to defend themselves and often won't go to court to press charges because they fear retaliation. They are "easy targets," according to Sergeant Bolte, who says: "The easiest persons you'll find to rob can't fight back or anything. If they're hit from behind they go right to the ground. It turns my stomach."

Detective Donald Gaffney of the robbery unit says: "We find some of them almost starved to death. They're afraid to leave their apartments after a robbery, and won't even go to the supermarket."

Most of the old victims live alone and endure the terror quietly. However, on October 7, 1976, Hans Kabel, 78, and his wife Emma, 76, natives of Germany who had lived in the same South Bronx neighborhood for more than forty years, hung themselves in their apartment. They had been robbed and brutalized there the previous October 2 and September 8. The Kabels left a note saying that they "could not live with the terror which is in this city."

Detective Thomas Sullivan of the robbery unit had met the elderly couple after the robberies. He said that Mrs. Kabel was terrified of going into the street and had not left the apartment in two years. "I tried to get them out of here," Detective Sullivan said. "I told them I could try to get them a different apartment but they said they wouldn't move."

Fires, many of them deliberately set by arsonists, are still another problem in the South Bronx. In October 1976 a fire swept through the Puerto Rican Social Club in the Morrisania section, leaving twenty-five people dead. Police suspected that the blaze resulted from a fire bomb thrown by someone who had a grudge against another person attending a party in the crowded club.

At the 42nd Precinct, which covers the southern part of the Bronx east of the Grand Concourse, Detective Anthony Mosca commented: "You wouldn't think you were in the United States when you see all the burned-out and abandoned buildings here. The only precinct that's worse is Fort Apache and that is adjacent to us."

But, of course, Fort Apache and the South Bronx *are* in the United States. Originally, however, the Missionaries of Charity came instead to the center of Harlem in 1971 in response to an invitation from Cardinal Cooke, Archbishop of New York, to Mother Teresa. Five Sisters were attached to All Saints Church on East 129th Street. Because they at first did not have a house, they lived in the Handmaids of Mary Convent on West 124th Street.

After a year in Harlem, the Sisters moved to Saint Pius Church on East 144th Street in the South Bronx. They lived in a house belonging to the parish on the same block as the church. But the houses on the block were eventually condemned and razed in an urban renewal project, leaving the Sisters homeless. On one of her visits to America, Mother Teresa asked Cardinal Cooke if he knew of a suitable house, but the Archbishop could think of none. With her characteristic vigor, Mother Teresa drove all over the Bronx looking for a place. She finally heard about a wrecked building owned by Saint Rita's Church on East 145th Street, off Third Avenue. The parish had been taken over by Augustinian Recollects in the spring of 1973 and they welcomed the help of the Missionaries of Charity. The building was renovated by the Archdiocese and the Sisters moved in in June 1973.

The quickest way to get to the convent from Manhattan is to take the express subway to 149th Street and Third Avenue. During the day this is a crowded, lively area with shoe stores, pizza parlors, banks and supermarkets, marked by the skeleton of an old elevated subway station.

As one walks south down Third Avenue toward the convent four blocks away, typical neighborhood sights come into view: the Bronx temple of the Seventh Day Adventists, the Tap Café, a blood bank, a South Bronx Model Cities office, Sylvia's Lounge, a dress factory with a sign saying "Experienced Operators Wanted; Payed Vacation," the *Iglesia Pentecostal de Salvacion*. There are hardware stores, used furniture stores, and a store with a sign advertising: "Sporting Goods and Police Security Guard Supplies." Shiny new cars are parked in the lot behind "The Godfather. Titrus Car Service by Appointment."

On the east side of Third Avenue and 145th Street are old houses and the Clark Junior High School. On the west side is an abandoned Sloan's furniture store on which colorful billboards are posted: *Gócelo en grande con V.O. Importado de Canadá"* and *"Esto y orgulloso de ser Puertorriquèno."* Next to Sloan's is an abandoned building littered with empty liquor bottles and trash, its crumbling walls painted with yellow graffiti: "Carlos . . . Latin Soul . . . Ricky."

The convent of the Missionaries of Charity adjoins this wreck. On the other side of the convent is another abandoned building, this one a gutted five-storey apartment house with a sign hanging in one of its doorways that reads, somewhat mysteriously, "Courtesy

Counter." The remainder of the block is occupied by a long, low, flat building with a cornerstone dated November 4, 1900. A sign identifies it as Saint Rita of Cascia Catholic Church and offers a schedule of Masses in English and Spanish.

Across the street from the church and the convent stand the red-brick blocks of a huge, neatly-maintained city housing project. The convent itself is a three-storey red-brick building surrounded by a tall wire fence. The gate leading to the doorway is not locked. Above the door is a small statue of the Virgin Mary.

I rang the doorbell on a gray November afternoon in November 1976 and was greeted by Sister Andréa, the young nun who is the superior of the convent. Although the Sisters are very busy, Sister Andréa had consented to make some time available to talk of their work.

The Missionaries of Charity observe their vow of poverty strictly. "To understand the poor, to serve them, you must be one of them," Sister Andréa observed as we sat down in the reception room. This small room, which doubles as a sacristy, is sparsely furnished with a Salvation Army chest, three chairs, and a table, all of wood. There is an autographed photograph of Cardinal Cooke on the wall and scores of photographs of youngsters the Sisters have helped.

Next to the reception room is a small chapel with two bookcases, a faded rug, and a small organ. Over the altar is a crucifix above which are written in capital letters the words of Christ on the cross: I THIRST. Behind the chapel is a combination dining room and community room and outside is a stone garden with a statue of the Virgin Mary. The sisters live on the second and third floors where they always have guests.

During my visit, four homeless women were staying at the convent as well as two "Come and Sees," young Catholic women who had expressed an interest in seeing the work of the Sisters and possibly joining the order.

Sister Andréa was born in Freiburg at the foot of the Black Forest in Germany. After reading about Mother Teresa's work, she joined the Missionaries of Charity in 1958 and was assigned to India. While serving as a nun she also obtained a medical degree. Sister Andréa found fulfillment in her work in India and resisted Mother Teresa's request that she transfer to New York as superior of the first convent in the United States of their order. But after a night of prayer and contemplation, she did agree to go and is now glad that she did. Sister Andréa at first felt uneasy because of the usual horror stories she had heard about crime in the New York ghettos and, as she put it, she experienced a "culture shock" upon her arrival. However, the experience has proved to be one that she would not have wanted to miss. "God works in strange ways," she says. She keeps up on her medical knowledge and hopes one day to serve as a practicing physician at one of the order's other missions.

During my visits in November 1976, five other young nuns were living at the convent. Sister Bernard is from Wisconsin and Sister Kathleen is from Syracuse, New York. Both of these Americans completed their novitiates at the Mother House in Rome before coming to the South Bronx. Sister Rochelle, Sister Joselette, and Sister Fidelia are Indians and completed their novitiates at the Mother House in Calcutta.

Spot also lives at the convent. He is a large, grayish dog with very few spots. One of the thousands of stray dogs who wander through the South Bronx, he was adopted by the Sisters after acid was thrown on him, and he now serves as a not very ferocious watchdog.

Sister Andréa told me that the Sisters rise each day at 4:40 A.M. After prayers and meditation, they attend Mass at Saint Rita's. Then they share a frugal breakfast and do their housekeeping and laundering. In keeping with their vow of poverty, each Sister has only two cotton saris; each day they launder one while wearing the other. In winter they wear second-hand sweaters and overcoats donated to them. Sister Andréa noted that the Indian Sisters had never seen snow before and had some difficulty before learning how to walk in boots instead of sandals.

After housekeeping, the Sisters go out each morning to give the love of Christ, service that takes many forms. They are not bound by any parish but travel all over the South Bronx and into Harlem. "Wherever we're asked, we go," Sister Andréa says. "Whatever we do, it is for God."

The Sisters always travel in pairs. They walk wherever they go, saying the Rosary and measuring distance by the time it takes to say one, two, three or more Rosaries. They walk in their saris through some of the most dangerous streets in the world. Muggings, and worse, happen frequently. But none of the Sisters has ever been harmed. "The Rosary is our protection," Sister Rochelle says.

On Monday and Thursday mornings the Sisters visit elderly shut-ins, many of them living now like virtual prisoners in their apartments because of their fear of crime. The Sisters do their washing, clean their apartments, give them massages when needed, and pray with them. "But mostly," Sister Andréa says, "they're happy as long as somebody is there to sit with them and talk with them."

The elderly have insulated themselves within a four-walled world far from the mainstream of society. And loneliness, while it is a condition not mentioned in any medical textbook, can kill as slowly as leprosy, especially when coupled with fear.

Sister Andréa recalls one old woman who had lived on the top floor of the same apartment building for thirty-five years. One day when she was alone a youth suddenly jumped in on her through an open window. He had somehow managed to let himself down from the roof and stole all of her money. When the Sisters arrived, they found the woman crying and trembling, so frightened that she wanted to move into the convent.

"It's such a pity," Sister Andréa says. "They have the feeling that nobody wants them. They're helpless, like children. We do whatever we can. The main thing is to make them feel wanted."

Other mornings the Sisters go out and give the love of Christ by visiting nursing homes, hospitals, and troubled families. Sometimes they will take members of these families into the convent. Often they are runaway teenage girls. Once it was an entire Haitian family whose mother had given birth to triplets.

On Saturday mornings, two Sisters visit the women's prison on Riker's Island, working with the Catholic chaplain there. "We help the inmates to pray," Sister Andréa says, "and tell them that God is with them, too." Often the Sisters will care for the families left behind while the women are in prison. They will give moral support to them during court hearings, which sometimes results in a reduction of bail.

Each day the Sisters return to the convent for a simple lunch, after which comes prayer and spiritual examination. Their afternoons are busy. On Wednesdays they go to the nearby Cardinal Hayes High School to take Spanish lessons so that they can communicate with many people of the parish who can't speak English. Twice a week the Sisters give sewing and cooking lessons to mothers of the parish. On Monday and Friday afternoons they hold classes on the Sacraments for children of the parish and give religious instruction on Saturdays. On Tuesday and Thursday afternoons they operate an after-school recreation center at St. Rita's.

In the summer, the Sisters conduct a day camp at St. Rita's. In 1976, 180 children attended the camp and were helped by eleven junior counselors and twenty-one volunteers. In winter, the streets around the convent are dark and usually deserted. But in the heat of summer they come to life with music from transistor radios and throngs of kids splashing in water from open fire hydrants.

"We try to help with the day camp," Sister Andréa says. "But there are some young people who stay out on the street all night in the summer. They seem to have nothing else to do. Sometimes they come up to the convent door and ask for food. I can't imagine what their family life is like. It's so important to take God into your family. He needs you first."

Every evening of the year the Sisters gather together in their small chapel for their Holy Hour. A different Sister leads the prayers each evening as they kneel facing the altar with the crucifix above it and the words: I THIRST. Then they dine together, discuss the day's activities, and prepare for another day of service to the poorest of the poor.

In their work in New York, the Sisters are aided by Co-Workers from all five boroughs. The Co-Workers join the Sisters in their visits to incurable patients and prisoners and help with their after-school programs in religious education, arts, crafts, woodworking and remedial reading. The Co-Workers take the children on trips and finance vacations of two weeks for some of them at summer camps.

On the second Saturday of every month the Co-Workers meet in Manhattan in the Holy Family Church near the United Nations for a time of shared plans for work and for prayer. Perhaps the Co-Workers will read a message of thanks from Mother Teresa, such as this one from the fall of 1976:

God love you for the love you have given and the joy you share with each other and with me. We give each other so much and receive from each other much more, and this is what being a Co-Worker is about: the ability to give and receive—to love and to be loved—to serve and to be served. This is all that Jesus is, and Jesus gives us this enrichment. We have to share with our own—in our home, in our communities, in our parishes, in the city where we live and in the world. This is what is meant: "God loved the world so much He gave His Son."

He still continues giving His Son through you and me. For He still loves the world so much. And this is the true Co-Worker—the one who allows God to

100

love the world by giving Jesus to you, and, through you, to the world.

Let us pray: Our Father, here I am, at Your disposal, Your child, to use me to continue Your loving the world by giving Jesus to me, and, through me, to each other and to the world.

Let us pray for each other that we allow Jesus to love in us and through us with the love with which His Father loves Him.

Even as the Co-Workers are meeting in New York City and helping the Missionaries of Charity in the *barrios* of the South Bronx, the same works of charity are being performed thousands of miles to the south. This is also in the Americas, in the *barriada* (slum) section of El Augustino in Lima, Peru and in the *Hogar de la Paz* (Home of Peace) which Mother Teresa established in May 1974. Mrs. Maurine Patterson, Vice-Chairman of the Midwest Co-Workers describes the work there:

"The 'Home of Peace' is a large, two-story building, Spanish style, with an open court in the center where peach and lemon trees grow and there is a vegetable garden off to one side. Attached in the rear is a large chapel which holds about four hundred people and a large auditorium. The plans for the latter are that it will be used to house mentally disturbed people and alcoholics.

"The whole complex is surrounded by a wall. It is set in the very famous area known as PARADA (stopping place) which is in the middle of the most crowded, most turbulent sector of the city.

"One side of the first floor is taken up with a kitchen, parlors, etc. The other side is for the sick adults who are bedridden and in wheelchairs. On the second floor are the Sisters' quarters: dormitory and chapel. On the opposite side live the children.

"The object of the Home of Peace from the beginning was to care for those whom no one else would help.

"The sick patients who are cared for here are destitute, homeless, family-less men and women who have no where else to go. The Sisters have learned that often people must be discharged from the government hospitals and have no place to go. The Sisters ask that they be brought to the Home of Peace.

"People lie sick and dying in the streets of Lima, and it is hoped that soon these too may be brought to the Home of Peace as soon as it is possible to secure an ambulance.

"The children who are cared for in the Home of Peace are mostly the abandoned, the crippled, mongoloid, spastic.

"At the moment there are about fifty-four elderly sick in the Home, each requiring individual care, and about the same number of children are being cared for.

"Seven Missionaries of Charity are now living in the Home of Peace. Two of these still go out every day to work in the *barriada* (slum) sector of El Augustino where they had first begun their work. Sister Anad, whose Hindu name means Joy, is a German medical doctor and Superior."

Lima, Calcutta, New York—the location makes no difference. The Missionaries of Charity go wherever they can serve the poorest of the poor. And it makes no difference to Mother Teresa to which religion those needing help belong. There are eight million Catholics among India's 654 million people. But Mother Teresa will help any Indian who needs it because she is doing it for God. In this, she is a small part of a tradition going back to St. Francis Xavier.

Wherever she receives help in her worldwide missions, Mother Teresa is deeply grateful for it. In October 1975 she visited the Washington-Baltimore area and made a pilgrimage along the same road traveled by Mother Seton from Baltimore to Emmitsburg. Later she attended Mass at the National Shrine of the Immaculate Conception. After the liturgy, Msgr. John Murphy presented her with the Shrine's International Women's Award. Patrick Cardinal O'Boyle introduced Mother Teresa and gave her a check to further her work. In her speech of thanks, she said: "The work of God needs both you and me. Let us together do His work, something beautiful for God."

Something beautiful is being done in the South Bronx, especially with children who are of such great concern to Mother Teresa. One Tuesday before Thanksgiving I met Sister Kathleen at 3:30 P.M. and walked with her from the convent to St. Rita's. This is where the Sisters hold their after-school recreation center. Boys and girls from the parish, many of them fourth- and fifth-grade students at the nearby Public School 18, came to the center in back of the church.

About twenty girls gathered in one large room with Sister Kathleen and a young "Come and See" who had worked with the Legion of Mary. Ten boys joined Sister Joselette, Sister Rochelle, and myself in another room. Our afternoon there began with Sister Joselette leading the boys in prayer as they stood with heads bowed around a pool table. The boys asked God to "make them good boys."

We all sat down at a large table where the Sisters

taught the boys how to fashion little turkeys out of pine cones, pipe cleaners, paper cut-outs for feathers, and Elmer's Glue. A few of the boys lost interest in the turkeys after a while and took to playing pool, drawing pictures, or wrestling with each other. But there was a definite atmosphere of joy in the room.

During a brief lull I asked Sister Joselette, who was born in Kerala, India, and had completed her novitiate in India, what had brought her here to the South Bronx in 1973. "Mother told me to go," she replied.

I asked Sister Rochelle the same question. She is also Indian. With white teeth flashing in a small brown face, she said: "The Holy Spirit brought me."

As the afternoon went on, Michael, aged 8, settled down to play chess with Sister Joselette. Another, larger boy concentrated on pool and avoided making turkeys. "I don't want one of them ugly things," he said. "They don't like look like a turkey, they look like Big Foot." Sister Rochelle mentioned that he attended a "special school," but came to the recreation center regularly. "One of the main reasons to have the center is to keep them out of trouble," Sister Rochelle said.

She told me that the Sisters gather these and other children together at 9:30 A.M. on Sundays and take them to Mass. The boys are obviously enjoying themselves at the center, and I ask some of them why. "I like the Sisters 'cause they're nice," José, aged 9, tells me. Michael, the chess player, says: "They're nice. They teach us to play and we play. We hear about Jesus on Saturday." I also overheard a serious conversation between Sister Joselette and William, aged 7. The Sister asked him what a sacrifice was. "When you don't want to do it, you do it," William replied.

Later I went to the adjoining room where Sister Kathleen was helping the young girls to make turkeys.

They were less noisy and showed more concentration than the boys. Sister Bernard and Sister Fidelia returned from making a visit to a shut-in in Harlem and joined in the fun. Sister Kathleen fashioned a small angel out of styrofoam, gold leaf, white cotton cloth, and Elmer's Glue, helped by Lisa and Elaine, both attentive nine-year-olds.

"These children are wonderful," Sister Kathleen told me. "They represent the future hope."

At last it was time for the children to go back to their homes and for the Sisters to return to the convent for Holy Hour. It was now dark as I walked back to the convent with Sister Kathleen. At the door, she smiled, said "Pray for us," and was gone.

I walked alone in the dark toward the subway, passing St. Rita's again. I had visited with six Missionaries of Charity. I wondered: Could only six be making any meaningful contribution here? This was a vast ghetto of rootless youngsters living in empty buildings, fields of rubble, drug addicts and muggers, and burnt-out shacks that made it look like somebody's revenge on America for some past sin. To me the answer was yes. Thousands of decent people also lived here, along with childen who represented hope. The Sisters were living proof that somebody cared about them, that God cared.

As I passed St. Rita's I looked again at its bulletin board with the schedule of Masses and read these words underneath the schedule:

JESUS FORGIVES AND HEALS
JESUS PERDONA Y CURA

I walked on and did not feel alone.

# 11
# The Small Things

The question of whether Roman Catholics in the United States care about the hungry of the poor nations is perhaps best answered by considering the results of Operation Rice Bowl.

Each week during Lent in 1976, many families in one hundred and thirty dioceses gave up one meal a day and contributed the dollars thus saved to a project of "sacrifice and sharing" sponsored by their bishops and directed by Catholic Relief Services. (The Director of Catholic Relief Services, for whose support Mother Teresa has always expressed deep gratitude, is now Bishop Edwin B. Broderick of Albany who succeeded Bishop Edward F. Swanstrom in November 1976. Bishop Swanstrom had been associated with Catholic Relief Services since it was started in 1943.)

Five million dollars was raised in Operation Rice Bowl, the overwhelming majority of it from ordinary families. The funds will be used for such diverse projects as hunger relief in Chile, parish food centers in Bangladesh, drought relief in Tanzania and Kenya, helping the victims of the civil war in Lebanon, earthquake relief in Indonesia, rice shipments in India, and self-help programs designed to increase food production in more than a score of countries. Twenty-five percent of the five million dollars given by American Catholics will remain within the diocese to help the poor and hungry in this country.

The poor and the hungry will unfortunately remain with us from the South Bronx to Calcutta and will need help. But in one of her talks to the Eucharistic Congress in Philadelphia, Mother Teresa said that the poor do not need our sympathy and pity but our love and compassion. Mother Teresa sees Jesus in "the distressing disguise of the poor"—the naked, the lepers, the starving, the unwanted are Jesus. To her, the poor have great dignity and give us much more than they receive.

She recounted some stories at Philadelphia. One was about a starving woman she picked up one night from a Calcutta street. In this condition, Mother Teresa herself thought that she would have made demands, said that she was hungry. But before dying, the woman only took hold of Mother Teresa's hands and smiled, a smile of grateful love. "She gave me much more than I gave her," Mother Teresa said.

She told of a Hindu family in Calcutta with eight children who had eaten nothing for days. Their eyes were shining with hunger when Mother Teresa brought them some rice. The mother took the rice and disappeared. She had gone to share it with a hungry neighboring Moslem family. "Her eyes were shining with joy when I left," Mother Teresa said, "because she could share her love with others." To Mother Teresa, this was "doing what Jesus does. She broke her bread. Broke the love of Christ and divided it."

At the Eucharistic Congress, Mother Teresa spoke of those who are not naked, homeless, or hungry, but unwanted. Asking "Where is your old father or mother?" she told of a visit to a nursing home in England. It was a comfortable, well-maintained home, but she saw not a single smile on the faces of the old people there. They were all looking at the door, waiting for visitors who never came. "Smiles generate smiles, just as love generates love," she observed.

To Mother Teresa, in satisfying the hunger of the abandoned to be loved, it is important to consider what the other person wants, not what we want or the good feelings that an act of charity may bestow upon us. We must see Christ in the other person. To Mother Teresa an act of charity is summed up exactly in this prayer of Cardinal Newman, which the Missionaries of Charity around the world say after they take Holy Communion every day: "Dear Jesus, help me to spread Thy fragrance everywhere I go. Flood my soul with Thy spirit and life. Penetrate and possess my whole being so utterly that all my life may only be a radiance of Thine. Shine through me, and be so in me that every soul I come in contact with may feel Thy presence in my soul. Let them look up and see no longer me but only Jesus! Stay with me, and then I shall begin to shine as Thou shinest, so to shine as to be a light to others. The light, O Jesus, will be all from Thee; none of it will be mine; it will be Thou shining on others through me. Let us thus praise Thee in the way Thou dost love best by shining on those around me. Let me preach Thee without preaching, not by words but by my example, by the catching force of the sympathetic influence of what I do, the evident fullness of the love my heart bears to Thee. Amen."

Mother Teresa is not a writer, a scholar, a theologian, a doctor, or a politician. She is a woman who started out alone in Calcutta, with nothing but her faith and her inheritance of a long Catholic tradition, to give the love of Christ as best she could. However, she has written this prayer: "Make us worthy, Lord, to serve our brothers and sisters throughout the world who live and die in hunger and poverty. Give them through our hands this day their daily bread, and, by our understanding peace, give them joy."

It is in this spirit that the Missionaries of Charity are working right now throughout the world, doing the small things, preaching Jesus without preaching.

*Library of the*
**CHRISTIAN CHURCH (DISCIPLES OF CHRIST)**
KALAMAZOO, MICHIGAN